REVISE BTEC NATIONAL
Sport
UNIT 2

PRACTICE ASSESSMENTS Plus⁺

Series Consultant: Harry Smith
Author: Jennifer Stafford-Brown

- -

A note from the publisher

These practice assessments are designed to complement your revision and to help prepare you for the external assessment. They do not include all the content and skills needed for the complete course and have been written to help you practise what you have learned. They may not be representative of a real assessment.

While the publishers have made every attempt to ensure that advice on the qualification and its assessment is accurate, the official specification and associated assessment guidance materials are the only authoritative source of information and should always be referred to for definitive guidance.

This qualification is reviewed on a regular basis and may be updated in the future. Any such updates that affect the content of this book will be outlined at www.pearsonfe.co.uk/BTECchanges.

For the full range of Pearson revision titles across KS2, KS3, GCSE, Functional Skills, AS/A Level and BTEC visit:
www.pearsonschools.co.uk/revise

Published by Pearson Education Limited, 80 Strand, London, WC2R 0RL.

www.pearsonschoolsandfecolleges.co.uk

Copies of official specifications for all Pearson qualifications may be found on the website: qualifications.pearson.com

Text and illustrations © Pearson Education Ltd 2018

Typeset and illustrated by QBS Learning

Produced by QBS Learning

Cover illustration by Miriam Sturdee

The right of Jennifer Stafford-Brown to be identified as author of this work has been asserted by her in accordance with the Copyright, Designs and Patents Act 1988.

First published 2018

21 20 19 18

10 9 8 7 6 5 4 3 2 1

British Library Cataloguing in Publication Data

A catalogue record for this book is available from the British Library

ISBN 978 1 292 25671 9

Note from the publisher

Pearson has robust editorial processes, including answer and fact checks, to ensure the accuracy of the content in this publication, and every effort is made to ensure this publication is free of errors. We are, however, only human, and occasionally errors do occur. Pearson is not liable for any misunderstandings that arise as a result of errors in this publication, but it is our priority to ensure that the content is accurate. If you spot an error, please do contact us at resourcescorrections@pearson.com so we can make sure it is corrected.

Websites

Pearson Education Limited is not responsible for the content of any external internet sites. It is essential for tutors to preview each website before using it in class so as to ensure that the URL is still accurate, relevant and appropriate. We suggest that tutors bookmark useful websites and consider enabling students to access them through the school/college intranet.

Introduction

This book has been designed to help you to practise the skills you may need for the external assessment of BTEC National Sport Unit 2. You may be studying this unit as part of the BTEC National Extended Certificate, Foundation Diploma, Diploma or Extended Diploma.

About the practice assessments

The book contains three practice assessments for the unit, but unlike your actual assessment each one has targeted hints, guidance and support in the margin to help you understand how to tackle them.

 gives you relevant pages in the Pearson Revise BTEC National Sport Revision Guide so you can revise the essential content. This will also help you to understand how the essential content is applied to different contexts when assessed.

 gets you started and reminds you of the skills or knowledge you need to apply.

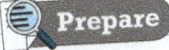 helps you on how to approach a task, such as making notes or a brief plan.

 provides content that you need to learn such as a definition, research method or analysis tool.

 reminds you of content related to the activity to aid your revision on that topic.

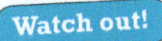 helps you avoid common pitfalls.

 appears in the final practice assessment to help you become familiar with answering in a given time and ways to think about allocating time for different task activities.

Before you undertake the research and each activity, read the support in the margin that accompanies each stage to ensure you take the guidance into account in your own responses. There is space for you to write your responses within this book. However, if you are carrying out research or writing notes, or simply require more space to complete your responses, you may want to use separate paper.

Example responses

Your responses to each paper will be individual, reflecting your own research and choices in relation to the task and activities. The section at the back of the book provides some guidance and examples of approaches to each paper, reflecting data available at the time of publication. The approaches, methodology, guidance and the way the data is used provides useful examples against which you can review your own work.

Check the Pearson website

For overarching guidance on the official assessment outcomes and key terms used in your assessment, please refer to the specification on the Pearson website. For this unit, check whether the assessment is completed on a computer. Check also whether you are allowed to take any notes into your supervised assessment, and any restrictions on the number of sides or nature of the notes, if so. Familiarise yourself with the breadth and range of tasks that are on the Pearson website in the Sample Assessment Material and any past papers.

The practice tasks, support and example responses in this book are provided to help you to revise the essential content in the specification, along with ways of applying your skills. The content of a task will be different each year and the format may be different. Details of your actual assessment may change, so always make sure you are up to date by asking your tutor or checking the Pearson website for the most up-to-date Sample Assessment Material, Mark Schemes and any past papers.

Contents

A small bit of small print

Pearson publishes Sample Assessment Material and the Specification on its website. This is the official content and this book should be used in conjunction with it. The questions have been written to help you test your knowledge and skills. Remember: the real assessment may not look like this.

Practice assessment 1

Revision task

Case study

> You should prepare notes in response to the information provided
> in the case study below.

Revision Guide
pages 84–86

Penny is 22 years old and works 10 hours a day as a nurse in a hospital. Her job involves a lot of time on her feet walking around her designated wards at the hospital to look after patients.

Penny takes part in exercise twice a week, playing netball with her village club. She plays once after work on a Wednesday evening and once on a Saturday morning.

The netball team have done well in their league and are going to be playing at a higher level in the next season. Penny is keen to improve her netball playing performance. She thinks if she is able to sprint faster she will be able to outrun her opponent to intercept the ball.

Penny decides to take part in training sessions to help to improve her netball playing performance.

Look at the six activities you need to complete for this revision task on pages 9 to 25. As part of your preparation for completing these activities, make notes and jot down your research below and on the next few pages. In your actual assessment, you may not be able to see the questions you will answer in advance, but they are likely to follow the model given here.

Research and notes

....

....

....

....

....

....

....

....

....

....

Prepare

Read the case study twice, then underline the key facts, such as Penny's age, how often she exercises, her job and her fitness goals.

Hint

Look for both positive and negative factors in the information you have been given, and identify areas that you need to research.

Hint

Penny exercises two days a week, and her job role is active as she is walking around all day.

Hint

Note that Penny takes part in netball on Wednesday and Saturday. You will need to be aware of this when planning a fitness programme for her.

Hint

Penny has identified that she wants to be able to sprint faster to intercept more passes. You will need to consider this when researching possible training methods.

Revision Guide
pages 84–85

Watch out!

For your actual assessment, ask your tutor or check the Pearson website to confirm whether you can take notes into your supervised assessment and, if so, whether there are any restrictions. Details of assessment may change so always make sure you are up to date.

Prepare

Make notes on **lifestyle factors and screening information** for a 22-year-old female. This should include BMI, waist-to-hip ratio, blood pressure and resting heart rate. You should also research and make notes on suitable lifestyle modification techniques.

Prepare

Penny is a nurse. You could use an internet search with key words such as 'nursing, stress, UK' to check whether this is a high-stress occupation.

Hint

Use bullet points in your notes to make them as clear as possible.

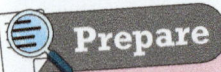

Prepare

Research the recommended daily calorie intake range for a moderately active 22-year-old female. You could look at www.nhs.uk and look for guidance on healthy eating.

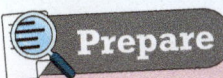
Revision Guide
pages 58–64

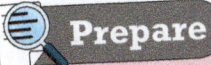
Prepare

For the **nutritional guidance** part of the task, you should find out the recommended intake of macronutrients and the sources of food Penny should eat to achieve the recommended calorie intake.

LEARN IT!

The **Eatwell Plate** was designed to illustrate what a healthy, balanced meal should look like, to help individuals make informed choices about what they eat. It is a model of what government nutritional experts think we should eat.

Prepare

Make sure you also research the recommended intake of water, units of alcohol and micronutrients.

Hint

Guidelines state Penny should be taking in approximately 2 litres of water per day. As she is a busy nurse, consider what strategies could be helpful to Penny if she needs to increase her water intake.

Revision Guide
pages 69–83

Prepare

Make notes relating to the different training methods and key aspects of designing a training programme for a netball player.

Prepare

Find and watch a video clip of a professional netball match. Make notes on likely fitness goals for a netball player, and possible areas of risk.

Prepare

Penny wants to improve her netball performance, possibly by being able to sprint faster. Note down what types of training will help with this goal.

Hint

The case study does not specifically state the component of fitness that needs to be trained; however, it is related to the ability to sprint quickly, so the component of fitness must be speed. Therefore, you should carry out research into different training methods that will improve speed, and any equipment these may require.

....

....

....

....

....

....

....

....

....

....

....

....

....

....

....

....

....

....

....

....

....

....

....

....

....

....

....

....

....

....

....

....

Revision Guide
pages 69–83

Prepare

Use this page to make further notes on different training methods and key aspects of designing a training programme for a netball player. In particular, make sure you use the FITT principles.

LEARN IT!

The **FITT** principles stand for:

- Frequency – how many times a week a person trains.

- Intensity – how hard a person trains.

- Time – how long the training session lasts.

- Type – the types of exercises or activities that are carried out in the training session.

You can use these principles as a structure to make notes about aspects of the training programme.

Prepare

There are other principles to consider. Check your notes or look at the Revision Guide and make sure you include these in your notes as well.

Revision Guide
pages 84–85

Hint

In order to complete the activities on pages 9–25 you should refer to your research notes as well as the further information provided in the lifestyle questionnaire. Make sure you read the questionnaire information carefully.

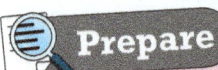
Prepare

The lifestyle questionnaire gives you more detailed information about the case study. Circle the new facts that will inform your analysis of Penny's relevant lifestyle factors.

Hint

With an active job and two sessions of netball a week, Penny leads an active lifestyle. You will need to bear this in mind when thinking about nutritional needs, as well as when designing a training programme for her.

Hint

Cross-check the information against your research notes. Highlight anything in your notes that will be useful when discussing the lifestyle factors relevant to Penny's occupation and relevant activity levels.

Hint

Remember that you can write on the assessment paper itself. You could make notes to yourself, ring or underline things you know you will want to refer to later.

Revision task
Lifestyle questionnaire

Refer to your research notes from pages 1–5 to help you answer the revision task that follows.

Section 1: Personal details

Name: *Penny Collins*
Address: *311 North Avenue, Parktown, PNO1 4AA*
Home telephone: *01854 6659852*
Mobile telephone: *07835 45381*
Email: *pennycollins@email.com*
Age: *22*

Please answer the following questions to the best of your knowledge.

Occupation

1   What is your occupation?
    Nurse

2   How many hours do you work daily?
    10 hours

3   How far do you live from your workplace?
    5 km

4   How do you travel to work?
    Drive

Section 2: Current activity levels

1   How many times a week do you currently take part in physical activity?
    Twice a week

2   What type of activity/exercise do you mainly take part in?
    Playing netball in a village league

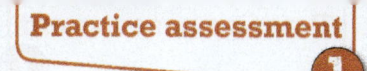
Section 3: Nutritional status

1 Complete the food diary for the previous two days.

Day 1	Breakfast	Lunch	Dinner	Snacks
Y/N	Y	N	Y	Y
Time of day	6.30 am	n/a	8 pm	11 am 3 pm
Food intake	Yoghurt	None	Salmon and salad with lettuce, tomatoes, peppers and sweetcorn	Apple Nuts Banana
Fluid intake	5 cups of tea, small bottle of water, 3 glasses of wine			

Day 2	Breakfast	Lunch	Dinner	Snacks
Y/N	Y	N	Y	Y
Time of day	6.30 am	n/a	8 pm	11 am 3 pm
Food intake	Small bowl of muesli	None	Chicken, boiled potatoes, peas, carrots	Orange Apple
Fluid intake	5 cups of tea, 1 can of diet cola, 4 glasses of wine			

2 Do you take any supplements? If yes, which ones?
No

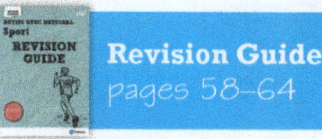
Revision Guide
pages 58–64

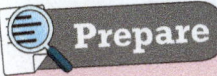 **Prepare**

Identify two areas for improvement in Penny's nutritional status and note possible alternatives.

Prepare

Penny doesn't eat lunch. This means no meal for $13\frac{1}{2}$ hours. Jot down two reasons why this could be a problem based on her goals.

Hint

Tea contains high levels of caffeine, which can help to improve concentration but can also make it difficult for a person to get to sleep.

Hint

Penny's snacks of fruit or nuts are high in micronutrients, which are beneficial to health.

Hint

Make sure you are able to identify which specific micronutrients are contained in different foods to help you to identify any vitamins or minerals Penny is consuming or that are missing from her diet.

Revision Guide
pages 47–48
and 53–57

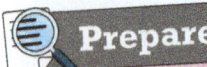 **Prepare**

How does Penny's alcohol intake compare with the guidelines in your research notes?

Hint

Stress can cause effects such as poor immune response, skin conditions, heart disease, stroke, angina, depression and stomach ulcers. Use your research notes to highlight possible stress management techniques you may want to suggest.

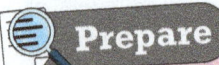 **Prepare**

Take a minute to look back at the notes you made about normative data for a 22-year-old female for blood pressure, resting heart rate, body mass index and waist-to-hip ratio. Jot the normative data down next to Penny's results. How do they compare? What might this mean for any training programme you design?

Hint

Speed and overall performance are the two components of fitness that need to be focused on for the training programme. The training should be specific to netball where possible.

Hint

Penny's goals are a very important consideration. You should keep these in mind when making any recommendations.

Section 4: Your lifestyle

Please answer the following questions to the best of your knowledge.

1   How many units of alcohol do you drink in a typical week?   *16*
2   Do you smoke?   *No*
    If yes, how many a day?   *N/A*
3   Do you experience stress on a daily basis?   *Yes*
    If yes, what causes you stress (if you know)?   *Work*
4   On average, how many hours sleep do you get per night?
    5 hours

Section 5: Health monitoring tests

Test results

Test	Result
Blood pressure	115/72 mmHg
Resting heart rate	68 bpm
Body mass index	18
Waist-to-hip ratio	0.7

Section 6: Physical activity/sporting goals

What are your physical activity/sporting goals?

Improve speed and netball playing performance

CLIENT DECLARATION
I have understood and answered all of the above questions honestly.
Signed: *Penny Collins*
Print name: *Penny Collins*
Date: *27.11.18*

You must complete ALL activities.

1 Interpret the lifestyle factors and screening information for Penny Collins.

....

....

....

....

....

....

....

....

....

....

....

....

....

....

....

....

....

....

....

....

....

....

....

Revision Guide
page 87

Watch out!

For your actual assessment, ask your tutor or check the Pearson website for whether you can take notes into your supervised assessment and, if so, whether there are any restrictions. Details of assessment may change so always make sure you are up to date.

Prepare

Spend 2–3 minutes jotting down a plan to structure your response. For example:
- Sleep: negative factor, less than guidelines
- Diet: negative factor, fewer calories than recommended, not balanced as per the Eatwell Plate
- Exercise: positive factor, already fairly active, non-sedentary lifestyle
- Smoking: positive factor, doesn't smoke
- Alcohol: negative factor, more than recommended level, explain potential impacts
- Stress: negative factor, stressful job, explain potential impacts
- Health monitoring test results.

Hint

Use the plan to start writing your response. Remember you have been asked to **interpret** the information – this means as well as describing the factors, you need to relate them to Penny and her health and well-being.

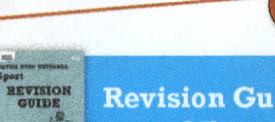

Revision Guide
page 87

LEARN IT!

Lifestyle factors include sleep, diet, exercise, smoking, alcohol, stress, sleep and the level of physical activity.

Hint

Identify positive **and** negative lifestyle factors from the lifestyle questionnaire. For each factor, state whether Penny meets the recommended government guidelines or not, the positive implications of this or the negative implications of this in relation to her health and well-being.

Hint

Useful sentence starters you could use are: 'One lifestyle factor is...', 'However, a positive lifestyle factor is...', 'The impact of this is...', 'Overall, Penny's lifestyle is...'.

Hint

One positive lifestyle factor for Penny is the level of her physical activity. With a job involving walking and playing netball twice a week, she already has an active lifestyle.

Hint

One negative lifestyle factor for Penny is her alcohol intake, which is above the government guidelines of 14 units per week for women.

(lines for written answers)

Revision Guide
page 87

Hint

Make sure you include all four health monitoring test results: resting heart rate, blood pressure, waist-to-hip ratio and body mass index (BMI) in your answer. Use the normative data tables in your research notes and compare these to the information presented in the lifestyle questionnaire.

Hint

As well as comparing screening information to the normative data, you should link the results to any potential health risks.

Hint

The systolic blood pressure reading is 115, within the normal range of 120–90 mmHg. The diastolic blood pressure reading is 72, also within the normal range of 80–60 mmHg. This is a positive lifestyle factor as it means Penny is less likely to suffer from illnesses related to having high blood pressure, such as a stroke.

Revision Guide
page 88

LEARN IT!

There are four main **lifestyle modification techniques** in the unit specification that you need to learn: strategies to increase physical activity, smoking cessation strategies, strategies to reduce alcohol consumption and stress management techniques. You could also highlight diet modifications.

Hint

You have been asked to **provide** and **justify** lifestyle modification techniques. This means you need to explain why you have made your suggestions, using information from the screening questionnaire and your research notes.

Prepare

You are less likely to forget anything in your response if you note down the key points you want to make. For example:

- Improve nutrition: more calories to increase weight and give more energy for training

- Alcohol reduction: strategies include more soft drinks, counselling, self-help

- Reduce stress: strategies include relaxation, breathing techniques, stress management classes

- More sleep: strategies include reducing caffeine, relaxation and earlier to bed.

2 Provide and justify lifestyle modification techniques for Penny Collins.

....
....
....
....
....
....
....
....
....
....
....
....
....
....
....
....
....
....
....
....
....
....
....
....

Revision Guide
page 88

....

....

....

....

....

....

....

....

....

....

Hint

Examine Penny's negative lifestyle factor: she is drinking more units of alcohol than recommended by the government per week. You should provide lifestyle modifications to support Penny to reduce her alcohol consumption.

....

....

....

....

....

....

....

....

....

Hint

Make sure you **justify** your recommendations. Penny should reduce her alcohol consumption because it may be contributing to her poor sleep and stress levels. As she does not excessively exceed the guidelines, minor lifestyle changes would probably be enough to address this.

....

....

....

....

....

....

....

....

....

Hint

Lifestyle modification techniques that can realistically be incorporated into Penny's everyday life should be included where possible. You can see that she drives 5 km to work each day. A healthier and realistic travel alternative may be to cycle to work each day. This will increase physical activity levels as part of her daily routine.

Revision Guide
page 88

Hint

Stress has been identified as a negative lifestyle factor. You should consider stress management techniques for Penny, such as going to an after-work yoga class that includes meditation.

LEARN IT!

Common barriers to change include time, cost, location and transport.

Hint

Make sure you have included the common barriers to change in your response, and identified those that may be relevant to Penny within your justification. As Penny works 10 hours a day, time may be a barrier for her. Have you acknowledged this in your response?

Hint

You should include a **conclusion** in your response that prioritises the different lifestyle modification techniques. Which would have the greatest impact on Penny's health? Which would be easy for her to implement?

3 Provide and justify nutritional guidance for Penny Collins to meet her specific requirements.

....

....

....

....

....

....

....

....

....

....

....

....

....

....

....

....

....

....

....

....

....

....

....

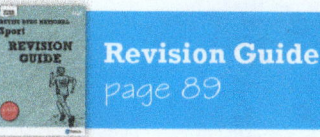

Revision Guide
page 89

Hint

The command words here are **provide and justify**. This means you need to give suggestions for how to amend Penny's diet, **and** explain why you have made those suggestions, using information from the screening questionnaire and your research notes.

LEARN IT!

The three **macronutrients** in a diet are carbohydrates, fats and proteins. The **micronutrients** are vitamins A, B, C and D and the minerals are calcium and iron. For each of these macronutrients and micronutrients you will need to know examples of food sources and use this in your guidance.

Hint

Refer to Penny's BMI and waist-to-hip ratio. Use this information and her food diary to work out if Penny is eating the right number of calories. Include the RDA calorie intake from your research notes.

Revision Guide
page 89

Hint

Use the number of marks and answer lines as guidance for how much to write and how long to spend on an activity.

Hint

Extra training sessions mean that Penny will be doing more exercise than at present. Make sure you provide for this in your nutritional guidance.

Hint

Penny consistently does not eat lunch. In your answer you should comment on the potential issues with not eating three meals a day. Penny's job as a nurse may make it difficult for her to find time to eat lunch. Your answer should address this barrier and make suggestions for how to make changes that fit into her lifestyle. For example, she could make lunch the day before or at the weekend for the whole week.

LEARN IT!

The guideline for **fluid intake** is 2–2.5 litres per day.

4   Propose and justify different training methods that meet Penny Collins'
    training needs.

....

....

....

....

....

....

....

....

....

....

....

....

....

....

....

....

....

....

....

....

....

Revision Guide
page 90

Hint

You are asked to **propose and justify** different training methods. You should relate any suggestions you make to Penny, her lifestyle, fitness levels and goals.

Hint

Penny's goals are to improve speed and her overall netball playing performance. You must ensure that any training methods you suggest are relevant to her goals.

Hint

Training methods should replicate the type of sport the person takes part in. Penny plays netball, which consists of periods of rest followed by high-intensity sprinting, along with rapid changes of direction. She would benefit from both physical fitness and skill-related fitness training.

LEARN IT!

Speed is one of the components of fitness Penny wants to improve. There are four different types of **speed training**: hollow sprints, acceleration sprints, interval training and resistance drills.

Revision Guide
page 90

Hint

Check your research notes for any fitness goals you identified as relevant to netball. What other training methods would be helpful? For example, agility and balance would be helpful in rapid changes of direction. Static and dynamic balance training can help to improve these. Coordination and reaction time are important in catching the ball. Reaction drills and ball-catching exercises would help with both coordination and reaction time.

Hint

Whatever training methods you recommend, make sure you justify these in relation to Penny and her needs and lifestyle. Penny is already fairly active so it is reasonable to include some high-intensity training. This wouldn't be the case for someone with a very sedentary lifestyle.

Hint

You should include any equipment that may be used in your selected training methods in your answer, describing how it would be used.

5 Design weeks 1, 3 and 6 of a six-week fitness training programme for Penny Collins.

Week 1

	Physical activity
Monday	
Tuesday	
Wednesday	
Thursday	
Friday	
Saturday	
Sunday	

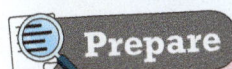

Revision Guide
page 91

Prepare

Before you start designing your programme, check your notes for the principles to apply and the types of training activities you identified. You could jot down what you want to include before you start allocating activities to days.

LEARN IT!

You need to know the **FITT principles** and apply them to designing your 6-week training programme. The FITT principles stand for:

- Frequency – how many times a week a person trains.
- Intensity – how hard a person trains; this will depend upon the type of training, such as percentage of maximum heart rate for aerobic endurance training.
- Time – how long the training session lasts.
- Type – the types of exercises or activities that are carried out in the training session.

Hint

Make sure you keep Penny, her goals and lifestyle in mind as you design the programme. Remember she works 10-hour days and already plays netball on a Wednesday and Saturday.

Revision Guide
page 91

Hint

A training programme should always contain at least one rest day a week to help the person's body to adapt and recover from the training. Make sure you write in 'rest day' rather than leaving the area blank.

Hint

You must ensure that your programme applies the **specificity** principle. The training must be matched to the needs and demands of the sport, in this case netball.

LEARN IT!

Fitness can only be improved by training above what you normally do. This is called **overloading**.

Hint

By week 3, Penny will have carried out two weeks of your training programme. Make sure that you build in sufficient **variation** to keep her engaged and motivated.

LEARN IT!

Max HR (or **MHR**) stands for maximum heart rate and **BPM** stands for beats per minute.

Hint

For any aerobic-based activity, you should give information about the heart rate Penny should aim for as either MHR or BPM.

Week 3

	Physical activity
Monday	
Tuesday	
Wednesday	
Thursday	
Friday	
Saturday	
Sunday	

Week 6

	Physical activity
Monday	
Tuesday	
Wednesday	
Thursday	
Friday	
Saturday	
Sunday	

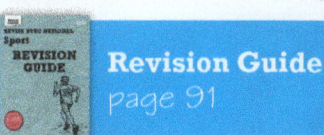

Revision Guide
page 91

Hint

Make sure your training programme shows **progression** so that the frequency, time and/or intensity of training increases over the course of the 6-week training programme. Use indications such as length of sessions, max HR or BPM to show this.

Hint

Check your response to Activity 4 and make sure that you have included all the relevant components of fitness that you identified in your training programme. Then check your research notes. Have you included everything you need to?

Hint

When you have completed all three training plans, look back over them and check the following:

• Have you incorporated the FITT principles?

• Is there sufficient variation?

• Is the training suited to the needs of the individual?

• Have you used the appropriate training methods outlined in Activity 4?

• Is there clear progression through the programme?

• Have you included suitable intensity levels for the activities?

• Have you allowed for rest and recovery?

Revision Guide
page 92

Revision Guide page 92

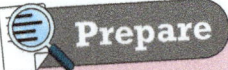

Hint

You are asked to **justify** your programme. This means giving the **reasons** for your choices.

Prepare

You should spend 2–3 minutes planning your response, either in your head or on paper. Jot down the key points you want to include to help you structure your response. These might include:

- application of the FITT principles
- application of other principles of training, such as specificity, overload, progression, rest and recovery, adaptation and variation
- individual needs
- penny's goals
- periodisation (macrocycle, mesocycle, microcycle).

Hint

Include Penny's training programme aims and objectives and her personal goals in your justification. Penny wanted to improve her speed and overall netball performance, so make sure you relate the training programme to these goals. You should also include information on the resources Penny will need to carry out the training programme in your justification.

6 Justify the fitness training programme that you have designed for Penny Collins.

....

....

....

....

....

....

....

....

....

....

....

....

....

....

....

....

....

....

....

....

....

....

....

....

....

....

....

....

....

....

....

....

....

....

....

....

....

....

....

....

....

....

....

....

....

....

....

....

....

Revision Guide
page 92

LEARN IT!

You should include SMARTER personal goals in your justification. **SMARTER goals** stand for:

- Specific
- Measurable
- Achievable
- Realistic
- Time-related
- Exciting
- Recorded.

Hint

You should give a justification that demonstrates relevance to the design of your training programme, such as the types of activities or exercises you have recommended and how these meet the training requirements of the individual.

Hint

Some useful sentence starters might be:

'This programme incorporates the SMARTER principle by...'

'It is achievable for Penny because...'

'Specificity has been applied by...'

'Overload has been incorporated because...'

Revision Guide
page 92

Hint

Your training plan should include specific types of training, as well as progression, variation, specificity, and rest and recovery. In your answer you should ensure that you explain how your programme has addressed each of these.

Hint

Your training plan should show **progression**. Explain how the progression occurs and link this to the aim of improving speed and overall performance. Progression could mean increasing the length of sessions, the weight lifted, the max HR or BPM.

LEARN IT!

Periodisation is a training cycle to make sure you are at peak fitness for the playing season or particular competition. The cycle can be a season, year or even four years, for example, a training cycle in preparation for the next Olympics. It may not be relevant to every individual planning a training programme, but you could consider it in your answer.

....
....
....
....
....
....
....
....
....
....
....
....
....
....
....
....
....
....
....
....
....
....
....
....
....
....

Revision Guide
page 92

....

....

....

....

....

....

....

....

....

....

....

....

....

....

....

....

....

....

....

....

....

....

....

....

....

....

....

Hint

If your training plan requires specific resources (for example, a netball, stopwatch, reaction balls, cones), make sure you explain what these are and how you have ensured that their use fits into the needs of the individual. For example, Penny could use the resources available at netball training to incorporate reaction-time training.

Hint

At the end of every assessment, if you have any time left you should go back and check your answers. Check that:

- you have answered every activity

- your writing is legible (cross out and rewrite carefully above any words that can't be read)

- you haven't missed any key points (for example, have you given a training programme for weeks 1, 3 and 6, and not accidentally missed one?)

- you have referred to relevant data in your answers (for example, giving normative data in your answer to Activity 1).

END OF REVISION TASK

Revision Guide
pages 84–86

Prepare

Read the case study and identify the key facts about Shelly that you need to bear in mind when carrying out your research. You could underline, highlight or circle them.

Hint

Shelly does not take part in any exercise. Her job role is sedentary as she sits down all day. The often-recommended minimum level of exercise for a 38-year-old female is 10 000 steps per day or 30 minutes of moderate intensity exercise five days per week.

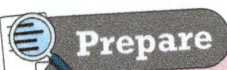
Prepare

Note down at least three headings you should use when structuring your research notes.

Hint

For a 38-year-old female, a healthy range of blood pressures would be 120–90 mmHg systolic and 80–60 mmHg diastolic.

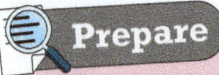
Prepare

Look at what you know about Shelly. Which of the common barriers to lifestyle modification could be relevant? Note down what these could be and some strategies to overcome these.

Practice assessment 2

Revision task

Case study

> You should prepare notes in response to the information provided in the case study below.

Shelly is 38 years old and works nine hours a day. She works as a scientist, which involves sitting down for long periods of time in front of a computer. She works flexible hours but must work a minimum of eight hours a day. This means she can start and finish work when she wants to.

Shelly doesn't take part in any sport or physical activity as it is not something she has ever really enjoyed. She used to like going for walks with friends but had to move away from them for her job. Since moving, Shelly has not yet found any friends to go walking with.

Some people at her work have suggested that Shelly may like to join a small team of scientists and enter a 5 km charity obstacle course fun run. Shelly is pleased to have been asked to join the team but doesn't feel that she is fit enough to be able to cover the whole 5 km distance.

Shelly decides to take part in training sessions to help prepare her to be able to join the team on their charity obstacle course event.

Look at the six activities you need to complete for this revision task on pages 34 to 50. As part of your preparation for completing these activities, make notes and jot down your research. In your actual assessment, you may not be able to see the questions you will answer in advance, but they are likely to follow the model given here.

Research and notes

....

....

....

....

....

....

....

....

....

....

....

....

....

....

....

....

....

....

....

....

....

....

....

....

....

....

....

....

....

....

....

....

....

....

....

....

....

....

....

....

....

....

....

Revision Guide
pages 44,
46–52, 55–57
and 86–88

Watch out!

For your actual assessment,
ask your tutor or check the
Pearson website for whether
you can take notes into
your supervised assessment
and any other restrictions.
Details of assessment may
change so make sure you
are up to date.

Prepare

Make notes on **lifestyle
factors and screening
information** for a 38-year-
old female desk worker.
This should include BMI,
waist-to-hip ratio, blood
pressure and resting
heart rate. You should
also research and make
notes on suitable lifestyle
modification techniques.

LEARN IT!

Body mass index is
calculated using the formula
$$\frac{\text{weight (kg)}}{\text{height (m)} \times \text{height (m)}}.$$

Hint

The case study does not
specifically state the area
of fitness that needs to
be improved. However, a
5 km run with obstacles will
require aerobic endurance
and muscular endurance.
Therefore, you should
research different training
methods that will improve
aerobic endurance and
muscular endurance that
are suitable for a person
that hasn't taken part
in any sport or physical
activity for a long time.

Revision Guide
pages 58–64

Prepare

For the **nutritional guidance** part of the task, you should find out the recommended daily allowance (RDA) for calories for a sedentary 38-year-old female, as well as the recommended intake of water, units of alcohol, macronutrients and micronutrients and the foods they are found in.

Hint

Strategies to improve nutrition include watching portion sizes, eating regular meals at appropriate times, eating more slowly and ensuring that the diet includes a minimum of five servings of fruit and vegetables a day.

LEARN IT!

Micronutrients are the vitamins and minerals that, although only required by the body in small amounts, are vital to healthy growth and development, disease prevention and well-being. They include vitamins A, B, C and D, and the minerals calcium and iron. Fruit and vegetables are good sources of many of these different micronutrients. Government recommendations are that a person should aim to eat at least five servings of fruit and vegetables per day.

....

....

....

....

....

....

....

....

....

....

....

....

....

....

....

....

....

....

....

....

....

....

....

....

....

....

....

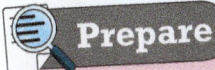

Revision Guide
pages 65–70

Prepare

Make notes relating to **different training methods** and key aspects of designing a training programme. Bear in mind what you know about Shelly as you do this. She wants to be fit enough to take part in the 5 km run with obstacles.

Prepare

Research the type of activities involved in a charity 5 km obstacle race. Note down the components of fitness involved.

Hint

Shelly may find her dislike of exercise a barrier to training. In the case study it states that Shelly used to enjoy being part of a walking group. Consider how this could be relevant to the training methods you research.

Hint

People new to running may take over 40 minutes to run 5 km. This requires aerobic endurance and muscular endurance. Aerobic endurance is required to help a person absorb, deliver and use oxygen and nutrients to produce energy for their working muscles. Muscular endurance enables the working muscles to be able to keep contracting for sustained periods of time.

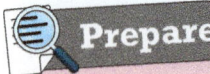
Revision Guide
pages 65–82

Prepare

Use this page to make further notes on **different training methods** and key aspects of designing a training programme for Shelly. In particular, make sure you have identified the main training principles to consider.

LEARN IT!

Types of training to improve aerobic endurance include **continuous training**, which is running at a steady pace for 30 minutes or longer, **fartlek training**, which is running at different speeds over different terrains, **interval training**, which is a work period followed by a rest period, and **circuit training**, which is using different exercise stations to develop aerobic endurance.

Prepare

Consider how the training could be tailored specifically for Shelly's 5 km event. Shelly has not taken part in any exercise for a long time. Note down how you will ensure she has a gradual introduction to running, as this is important.

Hint

Interval training could be used to allow for different periods of jogging and walking rests over the training weeks.

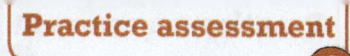
Revision task

Lifestyle questionnaire

Revision Guide
pages 84–85

Refer to your research notes from pages 26–30 to help you answer the revision task that follows.

Section 1: Personal details

Name: *Shelly Tann*
Address: *19 Valley Way, Big Town, BWO2 3AA*
Home telephone: *01234 56789*
Mobile telephone: *07911 23456*
Email: *stann@email.com*
Age: *38*

Please answer the following questions to the best of your knowledge.

Occupation

1   What is your occupation?
Scientist

2   How many hours do you work daily?
9 hours

3   How far do you live from your workplace?
4 km

4   How do you travel to work?
Bus

Section 2: Current activity levels

How many times a week do you currently take part in physical activity?
Zero

Hint

In order to complete the activities on pages 34–50 you should refer to your research notes as well as the further information provided in the lifestyle questionnaire. Make sure you read the questionnaire information carefully.

Hint

Shelly travels 4 km a day on the bus. Walking or cycling this distance could be an easy way to increase activity levels, especially as Shelly has flexible working hours, which means she could start later.

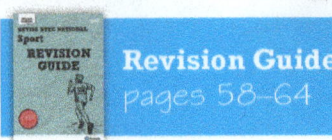

Revision Guide
pages 58–64

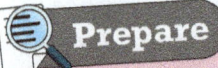

Hint

Shelly eats three meals a day and her food intake is quite evenly spread out.

Hint

Have a look at the types of foods eaten for most meals – most of them contain fried foods, such as chips, or have a high fat content, such as the cheeseburger.

Prepare

Most of Shelly's snacks have a high calorie content. Note down potential healthy swaps for each of these.

Hint

The current government recommendations are 14 units of alcohol or less per week for a female. A bottle of beer can be between 1 and 2 units, depending how strong it is.

Hint

A balanced diet contains lots of fruit and vegetables. This food diary shows that Shelly is only eating one portion of fruit and vegetables on each day.

Section 3: Nutritional status

1 Complete the food diary for the previous two days.

Day 1	Breakfast	Lunch	Dinner	Snacks
Y/N	Y	Y	Y	Y
Time of day	7.00 am	12.30 pm	7 pm	10.30 am 2.30 pm 8.00 pm
Food intake	Fried egg Sausages Bacon 2 slices of toast	Pepperoni pizza Chips	Fish and chips Peas	Crisps Chocolate bar 3 chocolate biscuits
Fluid intake	2 small bottles of water, 1 bottle of beer, 1 cup of coffee, 3 cups of tea			

Day 2	Breakfast	Lunch	Dinner	Snacks
Y/N	Y	Y	Y	Y
Time of day	7.30 am	1.00 pm	6.30 pm	11.00 am 2.30 pm 8.30 pm
Food intake	Two pieces of toast with butter and chocolate spread	Cheeseburger Chips	Chicken curry Naan bread Fried rice	2 chocolate biscuits Banana Crackers and cheese
Fluid intake	2 small bottles of water, 1 bottle of beer, 2 cups of coffee, 2 cups of tea			

2 Do you take any supplements? If yes, which ones?
No

Section 4: Your lifestyle

Please answer the following questions to the best of your knowledge.

1   How many units of alcohol do you drink in a typical week? *5*

2   Do you smoke? *Yes*

    If yes, how many a day? *20*

3   Do you experience stress on a daily basis? *No*

    If yes, what causes you stress (if you know)?

4   On average, how many hours sleep do you get per night? *8 hours*

Section 5: Health-monitoring tests

Test results

Test	Result
Blood pressure	*140/92 mmHg*
Resting heart rate	*85 bpm*
Body mass index	*25*
Waist-to-hip ratio	*1.0*

Section 6: Physical activity/sporting goals

What are your physical activity/sporting goals?
To improve aerobic endurance and muscular endurance to be able to take part in a 5 km charity obstacle course

CLIENT DECLARATION

I have understood and answered all of the above questions honestly.
Signed: *Shelly Tann*
Print name: *Shelly Tann*
Date: *15.11.18*

Revision Guide
pages 44–46
and 53–57

Prepare

Check your notes for the recommended alcohol intake for a woman. Jot down whether the value for Shelly is above or below this recommended weekly amount.

Prepare

Review each of the responses about Shelly's lifestyle. Note down which aspects can be seen as negative and what the health-related consequences are for each of these negative lifestyle factors. Are there any positive lifestyle factors in the responses? Think about the benefits to Shelly's health and well-being for each of these positive lifestyle factors.

Prepare

Use your research notes to compare these health-monitoring test results to normative data. Check your notes to see if these values are in the healthy ranges and if not, what the potential health concerns for Shelly are.

Hint

Think about what Shelly needs to achieve her goals.

Revision Guide
page 87

Watch out!

For your actual assessment, ask your tutor or check the Pearson website for whether you can take notes into your supervised assessment and, if so, whether there are any restrictions. Details of assessment may change so always make sure you are up to date.

Hint

Make sure you identify both positive and negative lifestyle factors from the lifestyle questionnaire. Factors that should be covered include sleep, diet, exercise, smoking, alcohol, stress and how much physical activity is undertaken. For each factor, state if Shelly meets the recommended government requirements or not and the positive or negative implications of this in relation to her health and well-being.

Hint

Shelly's sedentary lifestyle and a long working day were identified in the case study and confirmed in Section 1 of the lifestyle questionnaire, so you can use your research to help here. What other lifestyle factors have been identified through each section of Shelly's lifestyle questionnaire?

1 Interpret the lifestyle factors and screening information for Shelly Tann.

....
....
....
....
....
....
....
....
....
....
....
....
....
....
....
....
....
....
....
....
....
....

Revision Guide
page 87

LEARN IT!

BMI values can sometimes show a person as being overweight or obese if they have a high muscle mass. The waist-to-hip ratio will help you to determine if a high BMI is due to excess body fat or excess muscle mass, because if the person has a high BMI and a high waist-to-hip ratio you will know that it is excess fat. If, however, the person has a high BMI but a low waist-to-hip ratio, then the high BMI will be due to excess muscle mass.

Hint

Analyse the impact of the lifestyle factors you have identified. For example, is it a risk that Shelly's food is often fried? How might her lifestyle choice of smoking 20 cigarettes each day impact on her health and well-being? Is the amount of sleep she has each night appropriate for a 38 year old?

Hint

Consider whether any of the results from the screening information show areas of concern regarding Shelly's overall health and well-being. If any results do indicate clear health concerns, these should be discussed in your answer.

Revision Guide
page 87

Hint

You should link the health-monitoring test results with Shelly's health and well-being. Her high blood pressure may be due to her sedentary job, lack of exercise, diet and smoking. The blood pressure result indicates she is at increased risk of heart attack and other diseases.

LEARN IT!

A **waist-to-hip ratio** of 1 means that Shelly has too much weight around the middle of her body, meaning fat is stored around the internal organs such as the heart.

Hint

Make sure you discuss the potential health risks associated with Shelly's high waist-to-hip ratio.

2 Provide and justify lifestyle modification techniques for Shelly Tann.

....

....

....

....

....

....

....

....

....

....

....

....

....

....

....

....

....

....

....

....

....

....

....

....

Revision Guide
page 88

Watch out!

Make sure you consider all of the four potential areas for lifestyle modifications: strategies to increase physical activity, smoking cessation strategies, strategies to reduce alcohol consumption and stress management techniques. They may not always be relevant for every case study, but make sure you think about all four every time.

Hint

Aim for lifestyle modification techniques that can realistically be incorporated into the Shelly's everyday life where possible. She gets a bus to work each day. A healthier alternative may be to cycle the 4 km journey to work each day. This will increase her physical activity levels as part of her daily routine.

Hint

It is important to start any exercise with a gradual increase in progression. You could suggest that Shelly takes her bicycle on the bus and only cycles the last 2 km of the journey, gradually building up to the full 4 km cycle in to work when she is ready for that distance.

Revision Guide
page 88

Hint

Examine the individual's negative lifestyle factors. In this case study, Shelly smokes 20 cigarettes a day. You should provide lifestyle modifications to support her to stop smoking.

Hint

Make sure you **justify** your recommendations. Explain the potential negative health impacts of smoking as part of your answer.

Hint

Where there are several negative lifestyle factors, you should suggest a sensible prioritisation. For Shelly, stopping smoking could be the main priority as this is a negative lifestyle factor that is most harmful to her health. Increasing exercise levels might be her next priority to help to reduce the risk of associated chronic diseases and after this, addressing her diet as part of the overall approach.

....

....

....

....

....

....

....

....

....

....

....

....

....

....

....

....

....

....

....

....

....

....

....

....

....

....

....

....

Revision Guide
page 88

Watch out!

Stress has not been identified as a factor affecting Shelly's health and well-being. This is positive for her as stress has a number of negative effects on health and well-being, including depression and overeating. Be careful not to suggest lifestyle modifications that aren't needed!

Hint

Make sure you have included the common barriers to change in your response, and identified those that may be relevant to Shelly within your justification. Motivation may be a particular barrier. Have you addressed this in your response?

Hint

Ensure you summarise your recommendations, giving justification for the focus of modification techniques in terms of benefits or reduced risks to health.

Revision Guide
page 89

Hint

Include the RDA calorie intake from your research notes in this answer.

Hint

Refer to Shelly's BMI and waist-to-hip ratio to help you answer this activity, along with the two-day food and drink diary in the lifestyle questionnaire.

LEARN IT!

Shelly has low levels of fruit and vegetables in her diet. This probably means she is low in **micronutrients** such as vitamins A and C. Adding in fruits, such as apples and oranges, as well as green leafy vegetables and carrots, would help to address this.

Hint

Some of the Eatwell Guide recommendations include eating at least five portions of fruit and vegetables, having some dairy alternatives (for example, soya drinks) and choosing lower fat and sugar options. How might checking food labelling help Shelly to follow the Eatwell Guide?

3   Provide and justify your nutritional guidance for Shelly Tann to meet her specific requirements.

....

....

....

....

....

....

....

....

....

....

....

....

....

....

....

....

....

....

....

....

....

....

....

....

....

....

....

....

....

....

....

....

....

....

....

....

....

....

....

....

....

....

....

....

....

....

....

....

....

Revision Guide
page 89

Hint

Shelly eats foods that are high in fat and calorie content. She also eats few fruit and vegetables. Fruit and vegetables are the main source of vitamins and minerals in most people's diets. In your answer you should comment on the potential issues of eating high fat foods and not enough fruit and vegetables.

Watch out!

Don't forget to review Shelly's fluid intake. Do you think she is drinking enough to stay fully hydrated? Are there any concerns with the types of fluids she is consuming in relation to caffeine content?

Hint

Think about how Shelly is preparing her food. A lot of fried food means higher saturated fat content. Simple ways of reducing this would be to steam, boil or bake the food instead. A packed lunch could help address other issues in Shelly's diet, as well as reducing the saturated she consumes.

Revision Guide
page 90

Prepare

Spending 2–3 minutes jotting down the areas you want to cover in your answer will ensure you don't miss or forget anything important. Make a note of the key components of fitness that Shelly needs to improve so that you can go back to the list and check you have included training methods for each component listed. Use the space on this page to make yourself a short plan for your answer.

LEARN IT!

Aerobic endurance is one of the components of fitness Shelly wants to improve. You should know about four different types of aerobic endurance training:
continuous training, fartlek training, interval training and circuit training.

Hint

Shelly is going to be taking part in a 5 km obstacle course, so she will need to be able to keep jogging for the full distance, which will probably take at least 40 minutes. Consider what other skills she may need to tackle the obstacles along the way.

4 Propose and justify different training methods that meet Shelly Tann's training needs.

....
....
....
....
....
....
....
....
....
....
....
....
....
....
....
....
....
....
....
....
....
....
....
....

Revision Guide
page 90

....
....
....
....
....
....
....
....
....
....
....
....
....
....
....
....
....
....
....
....
....
....
....
....
....
....
....
....
....

Hint

Shelly's muscular endurance needs to be improved. Circuit training, fixed-resistance machines and free weights are options for training muscular endurance. There are also set principles for training muscular endurance, which include reps and sets and the rest period between each set.

Watch out!

Equipment will be required for main muscular endurance training methods so you should include this in your answer, describing how the equipment would be used. For example, circuit training could use weights or it could use body weight as a form of resistance to train for muscular endurance, such as step-ups onto a bench.

Hint

You need to **justify** your proposed training methods, giving reasons why they would be most appropriate for Shelly. For example, continuous training or fartlek training might be better than circuit training as these training methods more closely match what Shelly is getting fit for and can be run in a similar environment to the charity event.

Revision Guide
page 91

Prepare

Before you design your programme, check your notes for the principles to apply and the types of training activities you identified. You could write down what you want to include before you start allocating activities to days.

Hint

Remember – although the training needs to improve aerobic endurance and muscular endurance, it also needs to be **appropriate** for Shelly's lifestyle. As Shelly is a complete beginner, the training should be relatively easy to begin with. It also needs to be something she can maintain along with her current work requirements. Perhaps you can elaborate on the modifications you have already suggested for changes to activity levels, for example, cycling to work rather than taking the bus.

LEARN IT!

Aerobic training intensity is usually measured at percentage of heart rate max and should be in the aerobic training zone of around 60–70% max HR.

5 Design weeks 1, 3 and 6 of a six-week fitness training programme for Shelly Tann.

Week 1

	Physical activity
Monday	
Tuesday	
Wednesday	
Thursday	
Friday	
Saturday	
Sunday	

Week 3

	Physical activity
Monday	
Tuesday	
Wednesday	
Thursday	
Friday	
Saturday	
Sunday	

Revision Guide
page 91

Hint

Remember to apply the FITT principles to your training programme. Look back at page 19 for a reminder of what these are.

Hint

Over the six-week period you should ensure there is clear **progression** across your programme. This can be shown by increasing the frequency of training sessions, increasing the time for each training session and/or increasing the intensity of the training sessions.

Hint

By week 3, Shelly's fitness levels should have significantly improved. Make sure you apply the principle of **overloading** to increase the demands of your programme.

Hint

Referring to the needs of the individual, as provided in the case study and further information, will ensure that you are tailoring the programme appropriately. Remember that Shelly has not yet made new friends in the area. Have you ensured that your programme has some sort of social element that may help to maintain her motivation levels?

Revision Guide
page 91

Watch out!

Don't forget to include the additional principles of training in your training programme.

Hint

At least one rest day should be included per week to take into account rest and recovery, which gives the person's body time to adapt and recover from the training. Make sure you write in 'rest day' rather than leaving the day blank.

Hint

You know from the information in the case study that Shelly doesn't usually enjoy exercise. Variation is a key additional principle of training, which may help to keep her motivated. Think about other types of training that train the required components of fitness that may help Shelly to mix things up a bit, such as going for a run with another person rather than on her own or taking a different jogging route – these are simple ways to add variation but can make a real difference to a person's training session to help provide variety and interest.

Week 6

	Physical activity
Monday	
Tuesday	
Wednesday	
Thursday	
Friday	
Saturday	
Sunday	

6 Justify the fitness training programme that you have designed for Shelly Tann.

....

....

....

....

....

....

....

....

....

....

....

....

....

....

....

....

....

....

....

....

....

....

....

....

....

....

....

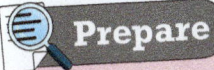

Revision Guide
page 92

🔍 **Prepare**

Create a quick plan for your answer. Note down the key points you want to include to help you structure your response. These might include:

- application of the FITT principles

- application of other principles of training, such as specificity, overload, progression, rest and recovery, adaptation and variation

- individual needs

- Shelly's goals and objectives

- periodisation.

Hint

You should include Shelly's personal goals in your justification, explaining how your training programme will help her achieve them.

Hint

The aim of the training programme is to develop Shelly's fitness so that she can have the muscular endurance and aerobic endurance to complete a 5 km obstacle course.

Hint

Objectives are how a person intends to meet their aims, so the objectives will be related to the types of training Shelly can undertake in order to help her meet her aim.

Revision Guide
page 92

Hint

You will need to justify how you have applied the FITT principles to the training:

- **Frequency**: explain how the number of sessions in the programme will develop Shelly's fitness. If they fit in with Shelly's work life she is more likely to fit them into her everyday routine.

- **Intensity**: explain why you have recommended an intensity for each exercise session. For Shelly to achieve 60–70% max HR she may just have to walk at speed. For resistance exercises, sets and reps should be included as well as the percentage of one rep max to show how heavy the weights should be. For example, for muscular endurance reps would be 10–15 and sets 2–3 with a percentage of one rep max at around 50%.

- **Time**: explain why you have recommended each training session time, where appropriate. The time spent training should usually increase over the six-week period as fitness builds.

- **Type**: you should include jogging in Shelly's training programme so that the muscles it requires are trained appropriately ready for the obstacle race.

....

....

....

....

....

....

....

....

....

....

....

....

....

....

....

....

....

....

....

....

....

....

....

....

....

....

Revision Guide
page 92

Hint

Remember to link your programme design back to Shelly, her aims and personal goals. You can refer to the points you made in earlier activities about the lifestyle modifications you have suggested and how the training forms part of this. You should show how your programme suits Shelly and her needs.

Hint

Your programme should take into account in Week 1 that Shelly currently undertakes no physical activity. Make sure you explain how and why you have done this. For example, you may have built in plenty of rest and recovery time.

Hint

Your programme should show progression across weeks 1–6. Explain what form this progression takes (such as amount of training time, or demand in terms of max HR) and how this helps to prepare Shelly for her goal.

Revision Guide
page 92

Hint

Resources should also be considered when justifying the fitness training programme. You should include details of what sort of facilities Shelly may need to access to complete the training, such as having to travel to a leisure centre to use gym equipment or using outdoor footpaths and cycle routes to travel to work. Equipment should also be included, which for Shelly will mainly be appropriate footwear for jogging and sporting clothing.

Watch out!

Make sure you look back at your research notes and the key elements for what to include in a training programme. Have you included everything?

END OF REVISION TASK

Practice assessment 3

Revision task

Case study

> **You should prepare notes in response to the information provided in the case study below.**

Raj is 27 years old and works eight hours a day as a personal trainer. His work involves visiting people's homes and delivering personal training sessions for each client. Sometimes the sessions he runs require him to take part in a lot of physical activity, such as going on a run with a client. Other times he is mainly involved with checking the client's exercise technique, such as ensuring they are lifting weights correctly, which does not require a great deal of exertion from him.

When he finishes a personal training session with one client, he cycles to his next client's house. The distances he cycles range from 0.5 km to 5 km. He typically cycles 15 km per day.

He usually has five clients booked per day, with each session lasting at least an hour.

Raj used to take part in weightlifting. His local area is hosting a weightlifting competition and he has decided he would like to get back into the sport and enter this competition.

> Look at the six activities you need to complete for this revision task on pages 59 to 75. As part of your preparation for completing these activities, make notes and jot down your research here. In your actual assessment, you may not be able to see the questions you will answer in advance, but they are likely to follow the model given here.

Research and notes

....
....
....
....
....
....
....
....
....

Revision Guide
pages 84–86

Prepare

Read the case study and identify the key facts about Raj that you need to bear in mind when carrying out your research. You could underline, highlight or circle them.

Time it!

It is important that you really understand the case study you are given. You should spend 5–10 minutes reading it and identifying key facts about Raj.

Hint

Raj takes part in a lot of exercise on a daily basis as part of his job. His form of travel is also active as he cycles to each of his personal training client's houses.

Hint

Raj's personal goal is to get back into weightlifting. This means that you will need to research training methods to build muscular strength.

Watch out!

For your actual assessment, ask your tutor or check the Pearson website for whether you can take notes into your supervised assessment and, if so, whether there are any restrictions. Details of assessment may change so always make sure you are up to date.

Revision Guide
pages 44,
46–52, 55–57
and 86–88

 **Time it!**

Time yourself when researching and making notes. You should spend no more than four hours doing so. The actual time allowed for research and making notes might vary. Check the latest guidance on the Pearson website.

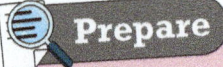 **Prepare**

Make notes on **lifestyle factors and screening information** for a 27-year-old active male. This should include BMI, waist-to-hip ratio, blood pressure and resting heart rate.

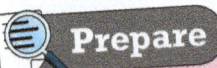 **Prepare**

You should research and make notes on suitable **lifestyle modification techniques**. Consider the requirements for weightlifting. What lifestyle choices would you expect Raj to make if he is to be successful and healthy?

Revision Guide
pages 58–64

Prepare

For the **nutritional guidance** part of the task, find out what the recommended daily allowance for calories for an active 27-year-old male is and put this information in your research notes.

Hint

You know from the scenario that Raj wants to take part in a weightlifting competition, which will require high levels of muscle mass. Foods that help to build muscle mass should be researched as these will be beneficial in his diet.

Hint

The amount of exercise Raj does each day varies depending on what he does with each client. Think about this when making notes about the nutritional guidance you may give him.

Hint

Create a list of strategies that could be helpful to a busy individual looking to improve their nutrition. This could include making and freezing meals in advance, using ergogenic aids and sports drinks.

Revision Guide
pages 69–83

 **Prepare**

Make notes relating to **different training methods** and key aspects of designing a training programme. Bear in mind what you know about Raj as you do this. He is already active and wants to take part in a weightlifting competition.

 **Time it!**

You should aim to spend one to two hours researching and making notes on this page and the following page.

Hint

The case study does not specifically state the component of fitness that needs to be trained. However, it mentions Raj taking part in a weightlifting competition, so one of the components of fitness must be muscular strength. Therefore, you should carry out research into different training methods that will improve muscular strength that are suitable for someone who takes part in regular exercise and who used to be a weightlifter, so has some knowledge of the strength-training exercises.

....
....
....
....
....
....
....
....
....
....
....
....
....
....
....
....
....
....
....
....
....
....
....
....
....
....
....
....
....

Revision Guide
pages 69–83

Hint

The purpose of a weightlifting competition is to lift heavier weights (relative to your body mass) than your opponents, therefore the more Raj can lift, the more likely he is to do well in the competition. This means Raj needs to develop his strength and power.

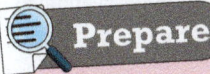

Prepare

Make sure you think about how the training could be tailored specifically for Raj's competition.

Prepare

Although you don't know a lot about Raj yet, you do know he is active, however currently his activity seems to focus on his aerobic fitness rather than developing his strength or power. Write down brief notes on the following:

- What is one objective he could set to help him achieve his aim?
- What personal goals could be set to help him achieve this in relation to his current lifestyle?
- What principles of training would Raj need to apply to improve his strength and power?

Revision Guide
pages 84–85

Time it!

You should review carefully any further information supplied to you. Spend at least 5–10 minutes reading the results of this lifestyle questionnaire before you start the activities.

Hint

In order to complete the activities on pages 59–75 you should refer to your research notes as well as the further information provided in the lifestyle questionnaire. Make sure you read the questionnaire information carefully.

Hint

Raj's job role involves taking part in lots of physical activity on a daily basis, which is a positive lifestyle factor.

Revision task
Lifestyle questionnaire

Refer to your research notes from pages 51–55 to help you answer the revision task that follows.

Section 1: Personal details

Name: *Raj Kanwar*
Address: *1 Waterbridge Way, Eastshire EF11 9ZZ*
Home telephone: *01987 65431*
Mobile telephone: *0791 192837*
Email: *raj@email.com*
Age: *27*
Please answer the following questions to the best of your knowledge.

Occupation

1   What is your occupation?
    Personal trainer

2   How many hours do you work daily?
    8 hours

3   How far do you live from your workplace?
    Varies – my clients live in and around my local area

4   How do you travel to work?
    Cycle to clients' houses

Section 2: Current activity levels

How many times a week do you currently take part in physical activity?

Every day – usually for around 3 hours a day when I am delivering personal training sessions to my clients

Section 3: Nutritional status

1 Complete the food diary for the previous two days.

Day 1	Breakfast	Lunch	Dinner	Snacks
Y/N	Y	Y	Y	Y
Time of day	6.00 am	12.30 pm	6.00 pm	10.30 am 2.30 pm 8.00 pm
Food intake	Porridge with blueberries	Large pasta salad with salmon	Mashed potatoes Small chicken fillet Boiled peas Boiled carrots Gravy	Banana Flapjack Apple Small bag of mixed nuts
Fluid intake	Orange and berry fruit smoothie, 1 litre of water, 2 strong coffees			

Day 2	Breakfast	Lunch	Dinner	Snacks
Y/N	Y	Y	Y	Y
Time of day	6.00 am	12.00 pm	6.00 pm	10.00 am 2.30 pm 8.00 pm
Food intake	Muesli and a banana	Large vegetable pasta salad	Vegetable curry with boiled rice	Apple Flapjack Two pieces of brown toast with jam
Fluid intake	Banana, kiwi and orange smoothie, 1 litre of water, 2 strong coffees			

2 Do you take any supplements? If yes, which ones?
Energy gels

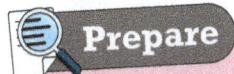

Hint

Raj eats three meals a day and has regular snacks, which are required to maintain his energy levels for the amount of physical activity that he takes part in.

Prepare

Look at the types of foods eaten and underline all that contain high levels of carbohydrates. Carbohydrates are a good source of energy. Now ring all those foods that contain high levels of protein. Raj's main goal is to increase his muscle mass. Consider whether his current diet contains the right balance of carbohydrate and protein to achieve this.

LEARN IT!

Energy gels provide high levels of carbohydrates, which provide energy for taking part in sports and physical activities that involve aerobic fitness and muscular endurance.

Prepare

Look at your notes to check how much water intake is recommended per day and compare this with Raj's intake. Is he drinking enough fluid?

Revision Guide
pages 48 and
54–57

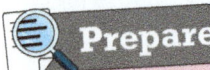

Check your notes for the recommended alcohol intake for a male. Is Raj's intake above or below this recommended weekly amount?

Review each of these responses about the client's lifestyle. Which aspects can be seen as negative and what are the health-related consequences of each of these negative lifestyle factors? Which factors are positive and will be beneficial to a person's health and well-being?

LEARN IT!

A person could have a high BMI because they have a lot of muscle tissue rather than excess body fat. The waist-to-hip ratio value will help you to work out if the BMI value represents high muscle mass or high levels of excess body fat.

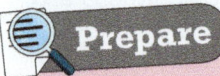

Note down two or three recommendations that will help Raj achieve his goals.

Section 4: Your lifestyle

Please answer the following questions to the best of your knowledge.

1   How many units of alcohol do you drink in a typical week? *5*

2   Do you smoke? *No*

   If yes, how many a day? *N/A*

3   Do you experience stress on a daily basis? *Yes*

   If yes, what causes you stress (if you know)?

Worrying if I will be able to get to my next client's house in time for their personal training slot and worrying if I will have enough time and energy to take part in my own weight-training session after work.

4   On average, how many hours sleep do you get per night? *6 hours*

Section 5: Health-monitoring tests

Test results

Test	Result
Blood pressure	120/80 mmHg
Resting heart rate	56 bpm
Body mass index	26
Waist-to-hip ratio	0.78

Section 6: Physical activity/sporting goals

What are your physical activity/sporting goals?

Improve strength to improve weightlifting performance and improve core stability to help to prevent injuries from weightlifting

CLIENT DECLARATION

I have understood and answered all of the above questions honestly.
Signed: *Raj Kanwar*
Print name: *Raj Kanwar*
Date: *20.11.18*

1 Interpret the lifestyle factors and screening information for Raj Kanwar.

....

....

....

....

....

....

....

....

....

....

....

....

....

....

....

....

....

....

....

....

....

....

....

....

....

....

Revision Guide
page 87

⏱ **Time it!**

You should spend around 30 minutes answering this activity. Make sure your answer covers both the lifestyle factors and the screening information provided in the further information.

Watch out!

For your actual assessment, ask your tutor or check the Pearson website for whether you can take notes into your supervised assessment and, if so, whether there are any restrictions. Details of assessment may change so always make sure you are up to date.

Hint

You need to identify both positive and negative lifestyle factors from the lifestyle questionnaire. Raj doesn't drink more than the guidelines and doesn't smoke. You should describe these as positive lifestyle factors for him.

Hint

Stress, diet and sleep are also lifestyle factors that should be reviewed. From the information provided in the lifestyle questionnaire you need to determine if six hours of sleep is sufficient for Raj's health and well-being.

Revision Guide
page 87

Hint

Look carefully at Raj's diet. He has an active job and wants to build muscle. Currently his calorie intake is not high enough to support him in both of these. This is therefore a negative lifestyle factor that you should review.

Hint

Raj's fluid intake is lower than the recommended guidelines. You should discuss the potential impact of this negative lifestyle factor on his health and well-being.

Hint

Raj takes part in a lot of physical activity as part of his daily life. You should discuss the positive impacts on his health and well-being of this lifestyle factor.

LEARN IT!

Potential negative health impacts of **stress** include hypertension, angina, stroke, heart attack, stomach ulcer, and depression.

Revision Guide
page 87

Hint

Raj's BMI score is in the 'overweight' category. However, given his waist-to-hip ratio, it is likely that this is due to muscle mass rather than fat.

Hint

Raj has a normal blood pressure reading, which will help to reduce the risk of developing a range of conditions related to high blood pressure. Make sure you include discussion of this as part of the review of the screening test results.

Hint

The resting heart rate of an average male is 70 bpm, but Raj has a resting heart rate of 56 bpm. You should consider what this means in terms of his cardiovascular fitness and also how it will be beneficial for his health and well-being.

Revision Guide
page 88

Time it!

You should spend around 30 minutes answering this activity. In your actual assessment, use the number of marks as a guide for how long to spend on each activity.

Watch out!

There are two command verbs in this activity. Make sure you give the information required by **provide** and **justify** the lifestyle modifications that you have selected, with evidence from research and the case study information given.

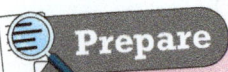

Prepare

Write down a short plan before you start writing your response. You might want to cover the following points:

- Reduce stress: strategies include goal setting, time management, positive self-talk, relaxation, breathing techniques, meditation, change to work–life balance.

- More sleep: strategies include reducing caffeine, relaxation and earlier to bed.

2 Provide and justify lifestyle modification techniques for Raj Kanwar.

....

....

....

....

....

....

....

....

....

....

....

....

....

....

....

....

....

....

....

....

....

....

....

....

....

Revision Guide
page 88

....

....

....

....

....

....

....

....

....

....

....

....

....

....

....

....

....

....

....

....

....

....

....

....

....

....

....

....

....

Hint

You need to suggest how to modify any negative lifestyle factors you have identified. For example, you know that Raj feels stressed worrying if he will get to clients on time or have enough time to train. What stress management techniques would Raj benefit from to help relieve this stress?

Hint

Examine the negative lifestyle factors of the individual. Raj only sleeps for six hours a night. For some people this may be sufficient, however, the average recommended amount is around seven to eight hours. Taking into account how much physical activity Raj takes part in, his body will probably need more time for rest and recovery, which is not met by six hours sleep a night.

Revision Guide
page 88

Hint

Lifestyle modification techniques that can realistically be incorporated into the individual's everyday life should be included where possible. Raj has time management concerns as he is worried that he won't have enough time to get to his next client's house and whether he will have enough time and energy to take part in his own training. He may need to consider an alternative location for his personal training, such as holding some sessions in a gym, so the clients come to him and he doesn't have to worry about travelling to them. Being located in a gym will also mean he is onsite to take part in his own strength training and will reduce the amount of cycling he needs to do on a daily basis, giving him more energy and time for his own training.

Hint

When you provide a lifestyle modification technique, you should provide justification for the focus of the modification techniques in terms of benefits to health as well as reducing risks of certain diseases.

3 Provide and justify your nutritional guidance for Raj Kanwar to meet his specific requirements.

....

....

....

....

....

....

....

....

....

....

....

....

....

....

....

....

....

....

....

....

....

....

....

....

....

Revision Guide
page 89

Time it!

You should spend around 20 minutes answering this activity. In your actual assessment, use the number of marks as a guide for how long to spend on each activity.

Hint

Include the RDA calorie intake from your research notes in this answer. The RDA should be for an active 27-year-old male.

Hint

Refer to Raj's BMI and waist-to-hip ratio to help you answer this activity. You will be able to work out if Raj is eating the right amount of calories from this information, as well as from looking at his two-day food and drink intake in the lifestyle questionnaire.

LEARN IT!

You will need to know about **ergogenic aids** that can be used to support a person's specific training programme. As Raj is looking to improve his strength, you should know about ergogenic aids that are high in protein.

Revision Guide
page 89

Hint

Raj eats three meals a day and at least three snacks a day. The types of foods he is eating are high in carbohydrates. Carbohydrates are a good source of energy for endurance sports. However, Raj wants to increase his strength, which means he will need to increase his muscle mass. Protein is needed in the diet to increase muscle mass. Protein is found in foods such as meat, dairy, soya and lentils. His diet contains very few foods that are high in protein.

He does eat a lot of fruit and vegetables and is easily meeting his recommended five-a-day, which is beneficial to health as these foods contain a large number of vitamins and minerals.

Hint

Fluid intake is important. Raj takes part in a lot of physical activity so he will lose water through sweating. The recommended daily intake of fluid for an average male is 2 litres per day, but more than this if the person is exercising.

4 Propose and justify different training methods that meet Raj Kanwar's training needs.

....

....

....

....

....

....

....

....

....

....

....

....

....

....

....

....

....

....

....

....

....

....

....

....

Revision Guide
page 90

⏱ Time it!

You should spend around 20 minutes answering this activity. In your actual assessment, use the number of marks as a guide for how long to spend on each activity.

LEARN IT!

Muscular strength is one of the components of fitness Raj wants to improve. You should know the principles when training for strength, including repetitions and sets, rest periods between sets, low repetitions and high load and pyramid sets as a method. You should discuss the training method as well as the body part being trained. For example, rather than saying pyramid sets for the upper body, specific body areas should be named, such as the shoulders, arms, chest, legs, back, etc.

Hint

We know that Raj is a weightlifter. Power is a component of fitness that would help to improve weightlifting performance, as it is the ability to produce a maximal force in the shortest period of time possible. Therefore, including training methods to improve power would be beneficial for Raj's weightlifting performance.

Revision Guide
page 90

Revision Guide
page 90

Hint

Core stability is another component of fitness that Raj wants to improve. There are a variety of methods of core stability training methods, including Pilates, yoga and gym-based exercises. Yoga has the added benefit of also being a method to manage stress as many yoga sessions have a relaxation period at the end of the session, so this may be beneficial to Raj for both core stability and stress management.

Hint

Once you have selected appropriate training methods for Raj, you also need to justify your choices, giving reasons why they would be most beneficial/appropriate for Raj. For example, yoga would help to provide relaxation to reduce stress as well as help with flexibility. This will help to return the muscles back to their original lengths after having completed weightlifting (which leaves muscles in a contracted state and eventually decreases flexibility).

5 Design weeks 1, 3 and 6 of a six-week training programme for Raj Kanwar.

Week 1

	Physical activity
Monday	
Tuesday	
Wednesday	
Thursday	
Friday	
Saturday	
Sunday	

Revision Guide
page 91

⏱ **Time it!**

You should spend around 15 minutes answering this activity. In your actual assessment, use the number of marks as a guide for how long to spend on each activity.

 **Prepare**

Before you start designing the programme, jot down quickly, on any blank space on this page, the key types of training you want to include and how you will show progression across the weeks.

Hint

The intensity of training related to weightlifting should be as a percentage of Raj's one rep max.

Hint

Remember that although the training needs to improve strength, core stability and power, it also needs to be appropriate for Raj's lifestyle. As Raj is not new to weightlifting and is already completing a lot of activity this needs to be taken into account.

Hint

Raj needs to be able to train alongside his current work requirements.

Revision Guide
page 91

LEARN IT!

You need to know the **FITT principles** and apply them to designing your six-week training programme. For **intensity** for weight training the weight lifted can be given as a percentage of the one rep max.

For weight training, specific body areas should be noted for the **type** of exercises or activities. For example, quadriceps instead of lower body. This makes it clear exactly what type of training is being carried out.

Hint

Over the six-week period you should ensure there is clear progression across your programme. This can be shown by increasing the frequency of training sessions, increasing the time for each training session and/or increasing the intensity of the training sessions.

Week 3

	Physical activity
Monday	
Tuesday	
Wednesday	
Thursday	
Friday	
Saturday	
Sunday	

Week 6

	Physical activity
Monday	
Tuesday	
Wednesday	
Thursday	
Friday	
Saturday	
Sunday	

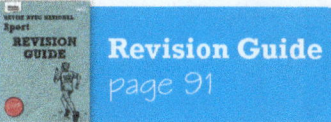

Revision Guide
page 91

Hint

Don't forget to include the additional principles of training in your training programme – at least one rest day should be included per week to take into account rest and recovery, which gives the person's body time to adapt and recover from the training. In weight training, people will usually train specific body areas on specific days, such as shoulders and chest on one day, and then legs and back on the next day.

Hint

Make sure you write in 'rest day' rather than leaving the area blank. For Raj, you will need to take account of his work commitments to ensure he has enough time for rest and recovery.

Hint

Variation is another key additional principle of training that helps the person avoid boredom. This can be accomplished by using different types of equipment, such as free weights and resistance machines in the gym, having a person to train with on some days or training in a different location, for example, outside with a weights set if the weather is good.

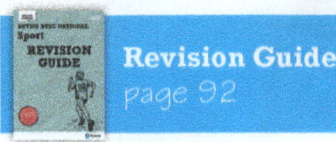

Revision Guide
page 92

You should spend around 35 minutes answering this activity. In your actual assessment, use the number of marks as a guide for how long to spend on each activity.

Hint

You should give a justification that demonstrates relevance to the design of your training programme, such as the types of activities or exercises you have recommended and how these meet Raj's training requirements.

Hint

Include the aims, objectives and personal goals of the training programme for the chosen individual in your justification. Raj wanted to improve his muscular strength and core stability to improve his weightlifting performance. Power would also be beneficial to improve weightlifting, so make sure you explain how the training programme would improve these components of fitness.

6   Justify the fitness training programme that you have designed for Raj Kanwar.

....

....

....

....

....

....

....

....

....

....

....

....

....

....

....

....

....

....

....

....

....

....

....

....

....

....

....

....

....

....

....

....

....

....

....

....

....

....

....

....

....

....

....

....

....

....

....

....

....

Revision Guide
page 92

Hint

You should explain how the FITT principles have been applied in order to achieve Raj's training goals.

Hint

In your answer you should give specific examples of where the programme has been changed over the course of the six weeks, justifying these changes to show application of FITT. For example, how there has been an increase in the amount of weight lifted by a particular muscle group, or holding specific core stability exercises for a longer period of time.

Prepare

Make sure you look back at your proposed training programme and include justification for each element. Update the training programme if you think you have missed anything out as you are writing your answer to this activity, as you may think of new ideas or need to add in a bit more detail in relation to the FITT principles in the training programme.

Revision Guide
page 92

Hint

You should also include in your answer the additional principles of training, which include specificity, overload, progression and individual needs, and how these are applied in the training programme to bring about the aims.

Hint

Individual needs are shown by explaining the starting weights for Raj, as these are heavier than a beginner would start with.

Hint

You can show that specificity has been applied through the use of training methods that are related to weightlifting, such as most of the training programme being related to developing muscular strength to help Raj prepare for a weightlifting competition.

Hint

In your answer you should state that Raj's training programme may need adapting to take account of periodisation when he knows the date of the competition.

....
....
....
....
....
....
....
....
....
....
....
....
....
....
....
....
....
....
....
....
....
....
....
....
....
....

END OF REVISION TASK

Revision Guide
page 92

Time it!

When you have finished answering all the activities, you should have a few minutes to go back over your answers and check that you have included all the key points. If you created a quick plan for your answer, you can check your answer includes all those points.

LEARN IT!

You should include SMARTER personal goals in your justification. **SMARTER goals** stand for:

- Specific
- Measurable
- Achievable
- Realistic
- Time-related
- Exciting
- Recorded.

Answers

Use this section to check your answers.

For the research and notes section of each revision task, we have included one example approach.

For the **activities** for each revision task, bullet points are provided to indicate key approaches and points, and the kinds of approach you could include in your answer. **Your answer should be written in an appropriate format** for each activity; this will usually be in full sentences, not bullet points. Your answers might include some of the points in the example answers, but not necessarily all of them.

> The tasks and sample responses are provided to help you revise content and skills. Ask your tutor or check the Pearson website for the most up-to-date Sample Assessment Material, past papers and mark schemes to get an indication of the actual assessment and what this requires of you. Details of the actual assessment may change so always make sure you are up to date.

Practice assessment 1

Pages 1–5: Research and notes

Page 1: Revision task

Prepare: You should underline the following parts of the case study:

> **Case study**
>
> Penny is <u>22 years old</u> and <u>works 10 hours a day</u> as <u>a nurse</u> in a hospital. <u>Her job involves a lot of time on her feet walking</u> around her designated wards at the hospital to look after patients.
>
> Penny takes part in <u>exercise twice a week, playing netball</u> with her village club. She plays once after work on a Wednesday evening and once on a Saturday morning.
>
> The netball team have done well in their league and are going to be playing at a higher level in the next season. <u>Penny is keen to improve her netball playing performance</u>. She thinks if she is able to <u>sprint faster</u> she will be able to outrun her opponent to intercept the ball.
>
> Penny decides to take part in training sessions to help to <u>improve her netball playing performance</u>.

Page 2: Research notes on lifestyle factors, screening information and lifestyle modifications

Prepare: Areas to research are exercise, diet, government recommendations and stress.

Normative health data for 22-year-old female

> You should have gathered information from reliable sources for body mass index (BMI), waist-to-hip ratio, blood pressure and resting heart rate. Examples are given below. Make sure you understand the information and what it means.

BMI

- Underweight: $<18.5 \text{ kg/m}^2$
- Healthy weight: $18.5–24.9 \text{ kg/m}^2$
- Overweight: $25–29.9 \text{ kg/m}^2$
- Obese: $30–39.9 \text{ kg/m}^2$
- Very obese: $>40 \text{ kg/m}^2$

High BMI increased risks: hypertension, infertility (female), osteoarthritis, sleep apnoea, type 2 diabetes, cardiovascular disease.

Low BMI increased risks: osteoporosis, amenorrhoea, anaemia.

Waist-to-hip ratio (women)

- Excellent: <0.75
- Good: 0.75–0.8
- Average: 0.8–0.85
- High: >0.85

Above 0.85 indicates too much weight around the middle, increasing risk of diabetes, stroke and heart disease.

Blood pressure

- Normal: 120–90 mmHg (systolic)/80–60 mmHg (diastolic)
- Hypertension (stage 1): 140–159 mmHg (systolic)/90–99 mmHg (diastolic)
- Moderate hypertension (stage 2): 160–179 mmHg (systolic)/100–109 mmHg (diastolic)
- Severe hypertension (stage 3): >180 mmHg (systolic)/>110 mmHg (diastolic)

High blood pressure increased risks: heart attack, stroke, kidney disease and vascular dementia.

Resting heart rate for women aged 18–25

- Athlete   54–60
- Excellent   61–65
- Good   66–69
- Above average   70–73
- Average   74–78
- Below average   79–84
- Poor   85+

Resting heart rate (RHR) improves with fitness – to lower RHR, increase fitness.

Government/health recommendations

- 14 units of alcohol maximum per week for a woman. Risks if drinking more than this: mouth, throat and/or breast cancer, stroke, heart disease, liver disease, brain damage, nervous system damage.
- No smoking. Risks of smoking: lung and other cancers, chronic obstructive pulmonary disease (COPD), stroke, heart disease.
- 10 000 steps per day or 30 minutes of moderate intensity exercise five days per week.
- Seven to eight hours of sleep per night and regular sleeping patterns. Poor sleep can cause: low immune system, heart disease, diabetes, poor mental health, stress, memory problems.

Demands of nurse as occupation

- Potentially high stress levels: research shows lots of articles linking nursing with high levels of stress.
- Long hours of work and walking around all day, so an active job.

Page 3: Research notes on nutritional requirements for a 22-year-old female

- Energy intake: female 2000 kcal a day, 2200 kcal if moderately active
- Caffeine: guidelines are up to four cups per day

Macronutrients

- Carbohydrate: 50–60% of the diet
  - Sources: sugar, fruit, bread, rice, pasta
  - Function: energy source
- Fat: 20–35% of diet
  - Sources: oils, dairy, butter, fatty meat, biscuits
  - Function: energy for low-intensity exercise, insulates the body, protection of internal organs
- Protein: 12–20% of diet
  - Sources: meat, fish, eggs, cheese, milk, beans
  - Function: growth and repair

Micronutrients

Vitamins
- Vitamin A (fat-soluble): 0.6 mg needed per day for women
  - Function: helps maintain good vision, healthy skin, hair and mucous membranes, and works as an antioxidant. Needed for proper bone and teeth development
  - Sources: liver, mackerel, whole milk, green leafy veg, carrots, orange-coloured fruits
- Vitamin B
  - Function: release of energy, aids production of red blood cells
  - Sources: lean meats, soya beans, leafy greens, fish, mushrooms, walnuts, eggs, cereal, wholegrains
- Vitamin C: 40 mg per day needed
  - Function: formation of collagen, works as an antioxidant, helps in healing, fighting infections and helps the body to absorb iron
  - Sources: citrus fruits, berries, green vegetables, peppers, tomatoes
- Vitamin D
  - Function: promotes strong bones and teeth
  - Sources: mostly sunlight, some in fish, cheese, egg yolk, fortified cereals

Minerals
- Calcium: 700 mg per day needed
  - Function: builds strong bones and teeth, normal muscle function, blood clotting
  - Sources: dairy foods, whole grains, fish bones, green leafy vegetables
- Iron: 14.8 mg per day for women
  - Function: needed for formation of haemoglobin in red blood cells, immune system, release of energy.
  - Sources: liver, meat, beans, nuts, dried fruits

Hydration
- Approx. 2 litres fluid in total per day for sedentary adult. Some of this will come from diet. Eatwell guidelines are six to eight glasses of water per day.
- Dehydration problems: impair strength, power and aerobic capacity.
- Needed for transporting nutrients, regulating temperature, digestive system.
- Fluid needed before, during and after event.
- Taking part in sports in hot climates requires an increase in fluid intake.
- Some fluid intake comes from fruit and vegetables.

Nutrition
- **Fruits and vegetables:** should make up a third of the food eaten each day. At least five portions should be eaten each day. Good sources of vitamins and minerals.
- **Starchy carbohydrates (potatoes, bread, rice, pasta):** should make up just over a third of the food eaten. High-fibre, wholegrain varieties should be eaten where possible.
- **Milk and dairy products:** around three servings per day of milk, cheese, yoghurt, for example; low-fat versions are preferable, for example, skimmed milk rather than full fat.
- **Beans, pulses, fish, eggs, meat and other protein:** two portions per day. Meat and meat products plus vegetarian meat substitutes such as Quorn or tofu.
- **Fats, oils and sweets:** eat only small quantities of foods from this group. This group includes foods containing high quantities of fats and oils, for example, butter, margarine, olive oil, cakes, biscuits, pastries, ice cream, cream and fried foods (for example, chips, burgers, etc.) and foods containing high quantities of sugar, such as fizzy drinks (not diet drinks), sweets, cakes, puddings, chocolate and jam.
- **Salt:** needed to maintain fluid balance. Too much salt may lead to high blood pressure and heart disease. High salt levels are found in processed foods, such as crisps, pre-prepared meals. An adult should eat no more than 6 g per day.

> Check government websites for the latest guidance on healthy eating. The Eatwell Plate is also known generally as the Eatwell Guide.

Pages 4 and 5: Research notes on training methods and designing a training programme

Prepare: Observations: short, explosive bursts of speed, quick turns, strength to throw ball longer distances.
Prepare: Components of fitness used in netball: aerobic endurance, muscular endurance, speed, reaction time, agility.

- **Physical fitness training methods:**
  Aerobic endurance training
  Continuous training (30-minute minimum): for example, running on footpaths and set jogging routes, flat terrain to ensure intensity remains similar.
  Fartlek training – jogging and running at different speeds for 30 minutes or longer, could run across different terrains, including hills to increase the intensity, and also include fast running as well as slower jogging.
  Interval training – fast running over set distances with slower jogging recovery periods.
  Circuit training – to include aerobic endurance stations such as skipping, jumping jacks, step ups, shuttle runs – exercise for at least a minute with minimal/no recovery time between each station.

  Muscular endurance training
  Low weights, high reps: for example, bicep curls 20 kg with at least 12 reps up to 20 reps using set resistance machines.
  Free weights: low weights, high reps using dumb-bells and barbells.
  Fixed-resistance machines: good for use by people who are new to weight training as less chance of injury.
  Body-weight muscular endurance training: for example, tricep dips, press-ups, squats, lunges.

  Speed training
  Hollow sprints: sprints for set distance, for example, 60 m with rest periods – for example, walk.
  Acceleration sprints: increasing speed from a rolling start, for example, jogging, to running to sprinting.
  Interval training: sprinting set distances with set recovery periods of lower intensity running or jogging.
  Resistance drills: using resistance, for example, parachute, sled or bungee cords to add resistance when sprinting.

- **Skill-related fitness training methods:**
  Reaction time training
  Reaction drills in response to a stimulus related to netball, for example, throwing the ball from a sitting position, or the person catching ball starts from a sitting position and has to stand up to catch it, or throwing a ball to a set spot that the catcher has to run to.

  Agility
  Speed, Agility and Quickness (SAQ) training – zigzag between cones. Improving balance also helpful through static and dynamic balance (Pilates, yoga helpful).

Equipment needed
- Speed training: resistance bands, parachutes, bungee rope, resistance tyres.
- Reaction time: stopwatch, whistle, visual stimulus, auditory stimulus, reaction ball.
- Agility: cones, whistle.
- Aerobic endurance: cardiovascular (CV) machines in a gym, outdoor track, outdoor terrain.
- Muscular endurance: free weights, fixed-resistance machines.

Training principles to consider for Penny

FITT:

- **Frequency:** For aerobic endurance this should be at least three times per week to have a training effect. Muscular endurance should also be carried out around three times per week. Penny is a busy nurse, so may struggle to find time to fit in training. Consider what types of training could be useful in limited time frame, or timings of the training to fit in with usual work commitments.
- **Intensity:** Needs to be sufficient to provide a training effect; for aerobic endurance heart rate has to be within the aerobic training zone. Aim for 119–140 bpm.

> 220 – age = max heart rate (max HR)
>
> 220 – 22 = 198
>
> 60%–70% max HR is in the aerobic training zone.
>
> Heart rate should therefore be around 119–140 bpm

  For sprinting interval training the work periods should be shorter and more intense as the training programme progresses, for example, sprinting shorter distances at higher speed or higher max HR. 80–100% max HR is 158–198 bpm.
- **Time:** Penny works 10-hour days, so may want to complete training for different components of fitness together. Could look to integrate her training into her travel to work each day, if not too far, such as jogging or cycling.
- **Type** of exercise: Netball uses a combination of jogging, running and sprinting so the type of exercise should include these types of activities. She also uses her arms to throw the ball, so muscular endurance may be required by the arms to improve netball performance. Speed has been stated as a component of fitness that needs to be improved, so types of speed training should also be included in the training programme.

Other:

- **Specificity:** Netball requires the following components of fitness:
  o Agility: being able to change direction quickly and precisely without losing balance to intercept the ball and also to pivot after having caught the ball to throw to a teammate.
  o Co-ordination: to run and throw the ball.
  o Reaction time: to be able to run quickly to intercept the ball from the other team.
  o Power: to jump high to try and intercept the ball or throw the ball at speed to a teammate.
  o Aerobic endurance: to be able to keep moving at a high intensity, to be able to run for the whole period of a netball match.
  o Muscular endurance: required in the legs to be able to repeatedly run for the duration of the match, and in the arms to repeatedly throw and catch the netball.
- **Overload:** Need to train more than 'usual'. Penny is on her feet 10 hours a day and plays netball twice, so is relatively fit. Sessions will need to push her further, so to increase aerobic endurance she will need to exercise in her aerobic training zone at least three days a week and progressively increase intensity or duration of training.
- **Progression:** She hasn't taken part in aerobic training before so she will need to start slowly, with possibly both jogging and walking for 30 minutes, building to just jogging over the training programme.
- **Reversibility:** Need to make sure training programme is realistic to prevent her taking too long a break or becoming injured. The frequency of training sessions needs to be sufficient to prevent reversibility.
- **Rest and recovery:** All training programmes need at least one rest day to allow the body to rest and recover. This rest day can allow for other types of activity, such as walking required in Penny's job, so a rest day may be taken on a working day.

- **Adaptation:** The cardiovascular and respiratory systems will start to adapt to the aerobic training by being able to take in and use more oxygen. The muscular and cardiovascular system will adapt to muscular endurance training through increasing the supply and uptake of oxygen to the muscle tissues.
- **Variation:** Need to ensure there is variation in exercise to prevent boredom. Runs could include changing the running routes, going with a friend, joining a running club. Muscular endurance can be carried out in a circuit training class, which helps with motivation as it is carried out as a group exercise activity. Methods to train inside should also be considered if the weather is bad, such as running on a treadmill, and this will also allow her to watch TV so could be more relaxing for her after a long day at work.
- **Individual needs:** Penny is active, busy, trains for netball two days a week, wants to improve performance and especially speed.
- **Periodisation:** Normally only considered by elite performers to make sure they reach peak fitness for the playing season and give the body time to recover during the off season, therefore this does not really apply to Penny.

Pages 6–8: Lifestyle questionnaire

Prepare: You may have circled 'distance from work' and 'drive as factors in the case study that inform your analysis of lifestyle factors.

Prepare: Two areas for improvement might be eating lunch and overall increasing carbohydrate (for example, wholegrain bread, rice/pasta).

Prepare: Two reasons might be (1) Penny wants to increase speed through extra training sessions, and (2) no lunch can mean not enough energy to fuel these extra sessions.

Prepare: Penny's alcohol intake is two units a week higher than guidelines (16 vs 14 units).

Prepare: Comparing data from notes with case study information produces the table below.

Test	Result	Notes
Blood pressure	115/72 mmHg	Both systolic and diastolic in normal range
Resting heart rate	68 bpm	In normal range
Body mass index	18	Underweight – need to increase calories
Waist-to-hip ratio	0.7	Excellent

Pages 9–11: Activity 1

Individual responses to interpret the **lifestyle factors and screening information** for Penny. The following provides example points only, against which you can review your own work. The response should have a well-written and logical **structure**, looking at all aspects of the information you have been provided with.

You should include both **positive** and **negative** lifestyle factors in your response using the screening information, and each needs to be described comprehensively. The lifestyle factors that should be covered are sleep, diet, exercise, smoking, alcohol, stress and physical activity levels.

Positive lifestyle factors

- Physical activity levels: Penny has an active job and is walking around for 10 hours a day. She also takes part in sport twice a week.
- Diet: low-fat diet.
- Smoking: does not smoke.

Negative lifestyle factors

- Diet: the food diary shows that she is probably not taking in sufficient calories for her energy expenditure. Not quite up to five fruit and vegetable servings per day.
- Alcohol intake: 16 units per week. This is two units above government-recommended weekly amounts.
- Stress: high stress levels from work.
- Sleep: only five hours sleep a night, which is less than recommended (around seven hours per night).

You should give a detailed analysis of the lifestyle factors identified for the chosen individual, leading to an interpretation of their impact on the individuals' health and well-being. The interpretation should have specific relevance to the health and well-being of the individual.

Analysis of lifestyle factors
Positive lifestyle factors

- Physical activity: high levels of physical activity will help to strengthen bones. The activities that Penny takes part in are weight bearing, so these will help to prevent osteoporosis. They may also improve posture, reduce risk of coronary heart disease (CHD), cancer and type 2 diabetes. In addition, they will relieve stress and reduce risk of depression.
  Netball is an activity that takes place with other people, so this will help to improve social skills.
- Diet: healthy food options selected – fish and lots of fruit and vegetables. Overall, a low-fat diet which gives a reduced risk of CHD.

Negative lifestyle factors

- Diet: low energy intake means she will have minimal fat stores and may not have sufficient energy levels to last the whole day. Very small breakfast and no lunch mean that she is likely to be very hungry. High amounts of caffeinated drinks – five cups of tea a day – leads to energy spikes and also potential to disrupt sleep.
- Alcohol intake: high levels of alcohol intake can lead to liver cirrhosis, stroke, hypertension and depression.
- Stress: high levels of stress can lead to hypertension, angina, stroke, heart attack, stomach ulcers and depression.
- Sleep: limited sleep can lead to depression and overeating.

You also need to undertake a detailed analysis and interpretation of the health-monitoring test results for Penny. The interpretation should be made specifically relevant to Penny and her health and lifestyle. All four health-monitoring test results should be covered: resting heart rate, blood pressure, waist-to-hip ratio and BMI.

Test	Result	Rating
Blood pressure	115/72 mmHg	Normal
Resting heart rate	68 bpm	Good
Body mass index	18	Underweight
Waist-to-hip ratio	0.7	Excellent

- Blood pressure and resting heart rate both not causing any concern: reduced risk of CHD and stroke.
- Low waist-to-hip ratio so she has low levels of body fat around the internal organs: reduced risk of CHD.
- BMI: underweight, not eating sufficient calories to maintain an appropriate body weight.

Pages 12–14: Activity 2

Individual responses to **provide and justify lifestyle modification techniques** for Penny. The following provides example points only, against which you can review your own work. The response should have a well-written and logical **structure,** looking at all aspects of the information you have been provided with.

Proposals of lifestyle modifications should be provided that systematically link to the lifestyle factor analysis you gave in Activity 1. The proposals given should demonstrate an understanding of significance, which includes the most important lifestyle modification technique and why.

Lifestyle modification techniques should demonstrate specific relevance to the individual's lifestyle and their requirements.

For Penny, the key areas you should discuss are:

Stress management techniques. Penny identified that she experiences stress daily. Nursing is a stressful occupation and stress can lead to chronic diseases such as high blood pressure, angina, stroke, heart attack, stomach ulcers and depression. Reducing her stress levels should help with addressing the other lifestyle factors identified below. Strategies to reduce stress could include:

- relaxation classes such as yoga – this could also help with sleep
- breathing techniques – could be carried out in lunch break or breaks in work to help to cope with stress in the workplace
- investigating what classes are provided at the hospital where she works to help with stress management, as if it is on site it will be easier to get to during a break at work.

Reducing alcohol consumption to 14 units per week or less (currently Penny consumes 16 units a week when 14 is the recommended maximum). Drinking more than the recommended weekly amount of alcohol can lead to liver damage, which is irreversible, and eventually lead to cirrhosis of the liver, which is fatal. It can also lead to stroke, high blood pressure and depression. Strategies to help with this would depend on whether Penny finds it easy to reduce her alcohol consumption or not, but could include:

- drinking a soft drink between each alcoholic drink; drinking wine spritzers rather than wine alone
- using an app to track her weekly alcohol consumption
- counselling
- self-help groups.

Increase calorie intake. Eating lunch to provide energy for the day and to help to bring BMI to normal levels. Suggestions could include:

- Penny doesn't have much free time to prepare a packed lunch so she could go to the hospital canteen to buy some lunch.
- Lunch should contain at least one portion of protein, such as fish or chicken, to help her muscles and body tissues grow and repair.
- She should include some fruit and vegetables to supply fibre to aid digestion and excretion of food and avoid constipation, as well as supply vitamins. For example, she could have a carrot in her lunch to supply vitamin A to help maintain good vision, healthy skin, hair and mucous membranes and to serve as an antioxidant. She could have a satsuma, which is quick to peel and eat and also supplies vitamin C, which is essential to fight infection. This would be very important for Penny as she works in a hospital, so is constantly surrounded by people who are unwell.
- She should also have some starchy food, such as brown bread, to supply energy to carry out her job as well as for any training she does after work.
- She could also eat more carbohydrates for breakfast, as currently she has a yoghurt, which is low in carbohydrates but high in protein – ideally a small bowl of muesli and yoghurt mixed together, as we know she likes both of these from her current nutritional programme.

Increase sleep. Lack of sleep could be causing health problems as well as reducing the energy Penny has for her chosen sport. Improving the amount of sleep could help with stress levels (although improving stress levels may also help with sleeping better). Strategies could include:

- reduce caffeine intake, by for example drinking decaffeinated tea

- try to go to bed earlier to aim for seven to eight hours' sleep a night
- try to take part in some form of relaxation technique such as breathing techniques while having a hot bath before going to sleep.

Pages 15–16: Activity 3

Individual responses to **provide and justify nutritional guidance** for Penny. The following provides example points only, against which you can review your own work. The response should have a well-written and logical **structure** and should demonstrate specific relevance to the individual's requirements.

The recommended daily allowance of **calories** for the individual should be stated and the fact that Penny has an active job role should be taken into consideration here. Quantities and sources of food for both **macronutrients** and **micronutrients** must be proposed, as well as **hydration**. The proposed nutritional guidance should be justified, making it specifically relevant to the individual's dietary requirements related to the food diary presented in the lifestyle questionnaire and the health-monitoring test results. Some key points are given below.

Calorie intake

- Energy intake for an adult woman should be around 2000 kcal per day.
- Penny has a very low BMI, in the underweight category, which shows she is not eating sufficient calories to maintain what is considered a normal body weight.
- Her active lifestyle means that the average daily number of calories of 2000 kcal per day may not be sufficient to meet the additional energy demands of her job; she therefore should consume more calories in order to maintain energy levels throughout the day as well as to be able to take part in the planned training programme.
- Increased calorie intake can come from having three set meals a day and healthy snacks.

Macronutrients

- Carbohydrate intake should be around 50–55% of the dietary intake.
  - Penny's food diary shows very few complex carbohydrates are eaten, just muesli and potatoes across both days. Increasing complex carbohydrates (such as brown rice, wholemeal pasta and bread) would provide sustained energy.
  - Foods containing simple carbohydrates such as apples should be increased. These would provide a quick release of energy.
  - Guidance is to increase carbohydrate intake. For example, wholemeal toast for breakfast with a yoghurt, sandwich for lunchtime.
- Protein intake should be around 15–20% of the dietary intake.
  - Protein is used for growth and repair of tissues.
  - Penny ate yoghurt, salmon, chicken and nuts, which are high in protein; however, she is not eating sufficient protein to meet the 15–20% suggested recommended daily amounts. Guidance is to eat more protein-based foods. Ideally two portions should be eaten per day, one at lunch and one at dinner. For example, have a sandwich with a meat filling such as chicken or turkey at lunchtime to increase protein intake.
  - As Penny has very little free time she could eat a protein bar as a snack as another way to increase her protein intake.
- Fat intake should be around 30% of the dietary intake.
  - Fat is used for insulation and storage of vitamins.
  - Penny has a very low-fat diet – only nuts and yoghurt consumed that contain fat.
  - She may not have sufficient body fat to store fat-soluble vitamins.
  - Low fat intake can also lead to a reduction in female hormone production, which can impact on the menstrual cycle.
  - Guidance is to increase unsaturated fat intake, eat more oily fish, hummus or avocado, as these are unsaturated fats.

Micronutrients

Penny eats a good amount of fruit and vegetables a day, which indicates she should be eating enough of the following vitamins:

- Vitamin A – found in the carrots and oranges she eats. Needed to help maintain good vision, healthy skin, and bone development.
- Vitamin B – found in chicken, fish and wholegrains (likely to be some in the museli). Needed to help release energy and produce enough red blood cells. Given Penny's busy job and additional energy needs for training she may still benefit from increase her intake, perhaps by adding leafy green vegetables and some more lean meat.
- Vitamin D – mostly from sunlight, but also found in salmon.
- Vitamin C – found in the orange, tomatoes, and peppers she eats. More vitamin C in the form of berries and more leafy green vegetables might be helpful given that Penny works in a hospital and will be exposed to lots of infections.

She is not eating quite the right types of foods to ensure she is eating the right amount of minerals. She needs to increase the following minerals:

- Iron – this is found in liver, meat, beans, nuts and dried fruit. Penny needs 14.8 mg per day so would benefit from increasing her intake. As she also needs to increase her protein intake, chicken sandwiches on wholegrain bread and snacks of dried fruit would help to increase iron intake.
- Calcium – this is found in dairy foods, wholegrains and leafy vegetables. Penny needs 700 mg per day and her food diary does not show sufficient intake of these foods (just yoghurt, milk with museli or tea). She should increase her calcium uptake, for example if she has the recommended chicken sandwich on wholegrain bread for lunch, this would improve her intake. More yoghurts and replacing peas with leafy greens for some evening meals would also help.

Hydration

- Penny's hydration levels may need increasing. Currently she drinks around six cups of tea or water daily, but also drinks wine, works in a warm environment and is active.
- Penny should increase her water intake to ensure at least 2 litres per day are consumed.

Pages 17–18: Activity 4

Individual responses to **propose and justify different training methods** that meet Penny's training needs. The following provides example points only, against which you can review your own work. The response should have a well-written and logical **structure** and should demonstrate specific relevance to Penny's training requirements.

You will need to state which methods of training would be most appropriate and why. In the lifestyle questionnaire, speed and improving netball playing performance are noted as the key components of fitness that Penny wants to improve. Some key points are given below.

Speed

To improve speed to intercept the ball there are a range of different training methods that could be used. These include:

- Hollow sprints: this training is similar to netball as there are periods of sprinting and then jogging or walking back to position.
- Acceleration sprints: this is also similar to netball as Penny may go from jogging to to full sprint to intercept a ball, so this would also be a suitable training method.
- Interval training: this can be done anywhere, with periods of high-intensity sprinting and then rest periods.

- Resistance drills: could include hill runs, or parachutes, sleds or bungee ropes could be used. Access to resources will determine if this method of speed training is going to be available to Penny.

Aerobic endurance

As a netball game lasts more than 30 minutes, increasing aerobic endurance will help to improve Penny's ability to run and jog around the court at high intensity for the duration of the game. Examples include:

- Continuous training: running/jogging at a steady pace for at least 30 minutes – can be carried out at lunchtime, before or after work.
- Fartlek training: this may be more appropriate than continuous training as it involves running at different speeds, which is something that Penny will be doing in a netball game rather than continuous running, which is all at the same pace.
- Circuit training: this involves stations with aerobic activities, usually performed in a group exercise class rather than on one's own, which may be more difficult to arrange around Penny's working hours.

Reaction time and agility

- Reaction and agility drills in response to an external stimulus.
- These should be netball-specific, such as sitting down and then getting up quickly to catch a netball that is passed to her.
- Agility drills could involve using a partner to dodge, cones on the netball court to move around and using the lines to run to in-between passing the ball to a partner.
- This would need to be carried out with a partner. Could be part of the netball training session so as not to take up more time as Penny does not have much spare time.

Pages 19–21: Activity 5

Individual responses to **design weeks 1, 3 and 6 of a six-week training programme** for Penny. The following provides example points only, against which you can review your own work. You will need to complete the tables provided for you.

For this activity you need to design a training programme that demonstrates specific relevance to all the fitness requirements for Penny, which are speed and overall reaction time.

The training programme should also demonstrate a thorough understanding of the principles of fitness training, in the context of the individual's lifestyle or training requirements. The FITT principle must be applied in full detail to the programme, and you should be specific about the intensity of the activities.

The training programme should have a range of activities to ensure there is variety to maintain interest levels and avoid boredom. There should be a progressive increase in intensity of how hard Penny should work over the six-week period as her body will adapt to the training and will be able to cope with higher levels of stress. Increases in exercise intensity are shown by increases in the percentage of the maximum heart rate that Penny works at for the aerobic training and increases in sprint distance and decreases in resting period for the speed training. There will also need to be progressive increases in intensity in order to overload the body systems so that they adapt to the training. Each training session should include types of training that are specific to train the required components of fitness identified to improve netball performance.

Additional principles of fitness training must also be applied, such as specificity, overload, progression, reversibility, rest and recovery, adaptation, variation and individual needs.

Not all of the additional principles of fitness training need to be applied here but the programme must demonstrate a thorough understanding of these and that they have been taken into account when designing the three weeks of the six-week programme.

An example is given below:

Week 1

	Physical activity
Monday	30 minutes during lunch break – hollow sprints 40 m sprints, 40-second recovery 10 sets, 80% max HR 60-minute yoga class after work
Tuesday	During lunch break Fartlek running – 30 minutes, varying intensity sprinting short distances, jogging, walking, keeping heart rate in 65%–85% max HR
Wednesday	70 minutes after work Netball 60–80% max HR Reaction time training
Thursday	60 minutes after work Acceleration sprints – 50 m sprints, 30-second recovery period 10 sets 80% max HR Reaction time training: interception skills with trainer or netball teammate
Friday	Rest day
Saturday	70 minutes 10 am–11.10 am Netball 60–80% max HR Reaction time training
Sunday	Afternoon Fartlek running – 30 minutes 80% max HR

In week 1, this programme is focused on introducing speed training (such as hollow sprints and acceleration sprints). 80% max HR is used to ensure that the training is giving enough challenge. Some training is incorporated into existing netball sessions to make best use of Penny's time.

Week 3

	Physical activity
Monday	60 minute yoga class during lunch break at work After work Circuit training – hollow sprints, reaction time and aerobic stations 1 hour 70–85% max HR
Tuesday	During lunch break Fartlek running – 35 minutes, 70% max HR
Wednesday	After work Netball, 60–85% max HR Reaction time training with a netball teammate
Thursday	After work Acceleration sprints 50 m sprints, 20-second recovery period 12 sets 85% max HR Reaction time training with a trainer or netball teammate – interception skills
Friday	Rest day

Saturday	70 minutes, 10 am –11.10 am Netball 65–85% max HR
Sunday	Afternoon Fartlek running – 35 minutes, 70% max HR

> In week 3, the programme shows progression through increasing the max HR and length of sessions.

Week 6

	Physical activity
Monday	60 minute yoga class during lunch break at work After work Circuit training – hollow sprints, reaction time and aerobic stations 1 hour 75–90% max HR
Tuesday	Lunch break Fartlek running – 35 minutes, 75% max HR
Wednesday	After work Netball, 65–85% max HR – reaction time training with a teammate
Thursday	After work Acceleration sprints with parachutes 60 m sprints, 20-second recovery period 12 sets 85–90% max HR Reaction time training with a trainer or netball teammate – interception skills, reacting to a stimulus
Friday	Rest day
Saturday	10 am–11.10 am Netball, 70–90% max HR Hollow sprint training with bungee ropes 50 m sprints, 30-second recovery Sets of 12
Sunday	Fartlek running – 35 minutes, 75% max HR

> In week 6, the max HR has increased again as well as adding in additional training on Saturday.

Pages 22–25: Activity 6

Individual responses to **justify the training programme** that you designed. The following provides example points only, against which you can review your own work. The response should have a well-written and logical **structure** and should show a thorough understanding of the principles of fitness training applied to the training programme.

The FITT principle must be justified in relation to the training programme and you should refer to the majority of the additional principles of fitness training, such as specificity, overload, progression, reversibility, rest and recovery, adaptation, variation and individual needs in terms of the training programme that has been designed.

You will need to give a justification that demonstrates relevance to the design of the training programme and the training requirements of the individual. In your response you will need to justify the aims and objectives of the training programme for the chosen individual as well as any personal goals and resources required. Some key points

related to the programme given in Activity 5 above are given below. Yours will differ according to the activities you include.

Penny's goals are to improve her netball performance, which includes her speed, reaction time and aerobic endurance. She is already fit, with a normal blood pressure and resting heart rate, so the training programme takes this level of fitness into account. She works 10 hours a day, so training sessions have been designed to fit in before or after work. She could also include the aerobic training as a method to travel to work, as it is a 5 km distance, which she could run. This would help to save time as Penny has a busy job working 10 hours a day so has very little free time.

Some key points are:

The FITT principles have been applied in designing this training programme:

- Frequency: training takes place six times a week.
- Intensity: intensity is sufficient to have an aerobic training effect for aerobic endurance as the maximum percentage heart rate is in the aerobic training zone. To improve speed, the distance covered in each sprint can be increased and the recovery time decreased to increase the intensity over the training programme.
- Time: time spent training from week 1 to week 6 increases from 30 minutes to 40 minutes for Fartlek training. This could be built up so that she could start running to or from work depending upon the times of her shifts. This will allow her to fit in her training as part of her daily routine and therefore would be more likely to maintain it even after the six-week training programme. The distance covered in speed training drills increases with reduced recovery time.
- Type: the activities all involve running, which is required in netball. A fast reaction time is also needed, so activities should help Penny to be able to react quickly to a stimulus such as trying to intercept another person throwing the ball.

Other principles of training also considered:

- Specificity: the reaction training is specific to netball, including interception drills, which is what Penny wants to improve.
- Overload: overload is provided by increasing the intensity and time in aerobic training. For sprint training, the distance sprinted and recovery time are reduced to produce overload effect.
- Progression: each week the time spent training increases and the intensity gradually increases from 70 to 90% for speed-related training and the intensity when playing netball increases from 65 to 85% to 70 to 90%, which takes into account the aerobic exercise and anaerobic exercise required in a game of netball to provide a gradual increase in progression.
- Reversibility: this should not occur, as there are sufficient training sessions to prevent this from happening.
- Rest and recovery: there is always one day a week that is a rest day to allow the muscles to repair and adapt from the training.
- Adaptation: the aerobic energy systems and cardiorespiratory systems should have adapted to the training and be able to cope with longer exercise periods and at higher intensity.
- Variation: the circuit training session can be varied from week to week with different types of stations to maintain motivation. Fartlek training can take place over different routes, such as cross-country, to maintain interest rather than just going round a running track.
- Individual needs: the reaction-time training and some speed training have been combined with the usual netball training nights as Penny works long hours and doesn't have much free time for training.
- In week 6, resistance has been introduced to increase the intensity and also to provide variation to maintain interest for Penny.

- Periodisation: This training plan is a mesocycle within Penny's macrocycle, and each exercise session is a microcycle of her annual training plan.

Resources:
- Fartlek training requires access to outdoor running areas such as pavements, cross-country routes or a running track. Penny will also need appropriate running shoes and sports kit.
- Reaction training will require a teammate or mates to provide the stimulus to react to, such as throwing the ball to set positions. They will need access to an area that is big enough to complete the activity, such as a netball court, gym or parkland.
- For the speed training, resistance has been added in week 6 so bungee ropes will be needed to provide this resistance – this adds variety as well as increasing intensity.
- Penny will need to be shown how to take part in the training so she could join a running club.

Practice assessment 2

Pages 26–30: Research and notes

Page 26: Revision task

Prepare: You may underline, highlight or circle the following parts of the case study:

> Shelly is 38 years old and works nine hours a day. She works as a scientist, which involves sitting down for long periods of time in front of a computer. She works flexible hours but must work a minimum of eight hours a day. This means she can start and finish work when she wants to.
>
> Shelly doesn't take part in any sport or physical activity as it is not something she has ever really enjoyed. She used to like going for walks with friends but had to move away from them for her job. Since moving, Shelly has not yet found any friends to go walking with.
>
> Some people at her work have suggested that Shelly may like to join a small team of scientists and enter a 5 km charity obstacle fun run. Shelly is pleased to have been asked to join the team but doesn't feel that she is fit enough to be able to cover the whole 5 km distance.
>
> Shelly decides to take part in training sessions to help prepare her to be able to join the team on their charity obstacle course event.

Prepare: Headings you could use include:

1 Normative data
2 Nutritional information
3 Potential training methods

Prepare: Common barriers to enjoyment that could be relevant and strategies to overcome these could include:

Lack of enjoyment of exercise – find exercise she enjoys, could combine with social activity to address no friends in new area.

Lack of energy/motivation if currently unfit – enjoyable exercise, ensuring achievable goals and good progression.

Possible lack of time – use flexible working hours to help with this.

Page 27: Research notes on lifestyle factors and screening information

Normative health data for 38-year-old female
BMI
- Underweight: <18.5 kg/m²
- Healthy weight: 18.5–24.9 kg/m²
- Overweight: 25–29.9 kg/m²

- Obese: 30–39.9 kg/m²
- Very obese: >40 kg/m²

High BMI increased risks: hypertension, infertility (female), osteoarthritis, sleep apnoea, type 2 diabetes, cardiovascular disease.

Low BMI increased risks: osteoporosis, amenorrhoea, anaemia.

Waist-to-hip ratio (women)
- Excellent: <0.75
- Good: 0.75–0.8
- Average: 0.8–0.85
- High: >0.85

Above 0.85 indicates too much weight around the middle, increasing risk of diabetes, stroke and heart disease.

Blood pressure
- Normal: 120–90 mmHg (systolic)/80–60 mmHg (diastolic)
- Hypertension (stage 1): 140–159 mmHg (systolic)/90-99 mmHg (diastolic)
- Moderate hypertension (stage 2): 160–179 mmHg (systolic)/100–109 mmHg (diastolic)
- Severe hypertension (stage 3): >180 mmHg (systolic)/>110 mmHg (diastolic)

High blood pressure increased risks: heart attack, stroke, kidney disease and vascular dementia.

Resting heart rate for women aged 36–45
Athlete	54–59
Excellent	60–64
Good	65–69
Above average	70–73
Average	74–78
Below average	79–84
Poor	85+

RHR improves with fitness – to lower RHR, increase fitness.

Government/health recommendations
- Maximum of 14 units of alcohol per week for a woman. Risks if drinking over this: mouth, throat, breast cancer, stroke, heart disease, liver disease, brain damage, nervous system damage.
- No smoking. Risks of smoking: lung and other cancers, chronic obstructive pulmonary disease (COPD), stroke, heart disease.

> You have not been given information in the case study about whether Shelly smokes or not. It may be helpful to ensure you have research notes on this and other areas, such as sleep, that could be useful.

- 10 000 steps per day or 30 minutes of moderate intensity exercise five days per week.
- Seven to eight hours of sleep per night. Poor sleep can cause: low immune system, heart disease, diabetes, poor mental health, stress, memory problems.

Problems with sedentary occupation
- Can increase risk of: poor immune system, poor sleep, depression, stress, poor flexibility/balance, osteoporosis, obesity, high blood pressure, coronary heart disease.
- Health concerns related to:
  o High blood pressure: can increase risk of heart attack, stroke, kidney disease and vascular dementia
  o Obesity: can be shown by a high waist-to-hip ratio. Excessive weight around the waist increases the risk for diseases such as CHD.

Lifestyle factors that you may need to consider
- Stress levels: whether Shelly has high or low levels of stress.
- Amount of sleep: is Shelly getting the recommended amount of sleep?

- Alcohol intake: is Shelly drinking less than or up to recommended units of alcohol a week?
- Smoking: negative effects of smoking. If Shelly doesn't smoke, this is a positive lifestyle factor.
- Shelly currently takes part in no physical activity at all. Government recommendations are moderate activity five times a week, moderate activity of 150 minutes across the week and activity for strength twice a week. No exercise increases Shelly's risk of serious health problems, including mental health problems, heart disease and obesity.
- Diet: is Shelly eating a balanced or non-balanced diet?

Lifestyle modification techniques for any identified negative lifestyle factors

- Managing stress: exercise, sleep, stop smoking, reduce alcohol, assertiveness, work–life balance changes, alternative therapies, meditation, breathing techniques, relaxation, time management, goal setting.
- Stopping smoking: nicotine replacement therapy, NHS smoking helplines, NHS smoking services, acupuncture, Quit Kit support pack.
- Reducing alcohol intake: break habits, 'dry' days, pace drinking, space out drinks, drink with food, self-help groups such as AA, cognitive behavioural therapy, alternative treatments such as meditation, yoga, acupuncture, hypnotherapy.
- Increasing physical activity: overcome barriers, build gradually, find activity that is enjoyable.
- Increasing amount of sleep: good sleep hygiene, earlier bedtime, no screens, relaxation.

Page 28: Research notes on nutritional requirements for a 38-year-old female

- Energy intake: female, 2000 kcal a day. More calories would indicate a positive energy balance, which can lead to weight gain. Fewer calories than this would indicate a negative energy balance, which will lead to weight loss.
- Activity levels will increase the number of calories required on a daily basis. Shelly has an inactive job so will not require more than 2000 kcal on a daily basis.
- Caffeine: guidelines are up to four cups per day. Caffeine is a stimulant so it increases a person's heart rate and increases alertness, so can make a person feel more awake and less tired, so may be useful to Shelly when she is working through complex scientific calculations.

Macronutrients

- Carbohydrate: 50–60% of the diet.
  o Function: provides energy source for sport.
  o Sources: sugar, fruit, bread, rice, pasta.
- Fat: 20–35% of diet.
  o Function: provides energy for low-intensity exercise, insulates the body, protection of internal organs
  o Sources: oils, dairy, butter, fatty meat, biscuits.
- Protein: 12–20% of diet.
  o Function: growth and repair.
  o Sources: meat, fish, eggs, cheese, milk, beans.

Micronutrients

Shelly has a poor overall diet and would benefit from increasing her intake of almost all vitamins and minerals. She needs to increase intake of:

- Vitamin A – 0.6mg per day needed for Shelly to help maintain good vision, healthy skin and for good bone development. Found in liver, mackerel, whole milk, green leafy veg, carrots and orange-coloured fruit.
- Vitamin B – needed to help release energy and produce enough red blood cells. As Shelly is going to need a lot more energy for her training, she should increase her intake of lean

meats, soya beans, leafy greens, fish, mushrooms, eggs or wholegrains.
- Vitamin C – Shelly needs 40 mg per day to help with healing, fighting infections and to help absorb iron. Found in citrus fruit, tomatoes, berries, and peppers.

Shelly should be getting enough vitamin D from sunlight, but she could increase her intake by eating more fish, cheese or fortified cereals.

She is not eating the right types of foods to ensure she is eating the right amount of minerals. She needs to increase the following minerals:

- Iron – this is found in liver, meat, beans, nuts and dried fruit. Shelly needs 14.8 mg per day so would benefit from increasing her intake.
- Calcium – this is found in dairy foods, wholegrains and leafy vegetables. Shelly needs 700 mg per day and her food diary does not show sufficient intake of these foods. She should increase her calcium uptake, for example by eating wholegrain cereal with whole milk, and green leafy vegetables.

Hydration

- Approximately 2 litres of fluid in total per day for a sedentary adult. Some of this will come from diet. Eatwell guidelines are six to eight glasses of water per day.
- Dehydration problems: impairs strength, power and aerobic capacity.
- Needed for transporting nutrients, regulating temperature, digestive system.
- Fluid needed before, during and after event.
- Some fluid intake comes from fruit and vegetables.

Nutrition

- **Fruits and vegetables:** should make up a third of the food eaten each day. At least five portions should be eaten each day. Good sources of vitamins and minerals.
- **Starchy carbohydrates (potatoes, bread, rice, pasta):** should make up just over a third of the food eaten. High-fibre, wholegrain varieties should be eaten where possible.
- **Milk and dairy products:** around three servings per day of milk, cheese, yoghurt, etc.; low-fat versions are preferable, for example, skimmed milk rather than full fat.
- **Beans, pulses, fish, eggs, meat and other protein:** two portions per day. Meat and meat products plus vegetarian meat substitutes such as Quorn or tofu.
- **Fats, oils and sweets:** eat only small quantities of foods from this group. This group includes foods containing high quantities of fats and oils, for example, butter, margarine, olive oil, cakes, biscuits, pastries, ice cream, cream and fried foods such as chips, burgers, etc., and foods containing high quantities of sugar, such as fizzy drinks (not diet drinks), sweets, cakes, puddings, chocolate and jam.
- **Salt:** needed to maintain fluid balance – too much salt can lead to high blood pressure and heart disease. High salt levels in processed foods, such as crisps, pre-prepared meals. An adult should eat no more than 6 g per day.

Pages 29–30: Research notes on training methods and designing a training programme

Prepare: Requirements for a 5 km obstacle course could include:

- Aerobic endurance in order to jog the 5 km distance.
- Muscular endurance in order for leg muscles to be able to keep contracting for long periods of time to complete the 5 km distance.
- Other muscles of the body may be required in an obstacle course in order to climb up and over obstacles such as a high wall. Therefore, the upper body muscles will also require training to be able to help lift Shelly over and through obstacles.

Suitable training options

Aerobic endurance

- Continuous training: steady pace for a minimum of 30 minutes. Shelly can do this by walking at speed, jogging or cycling.
- Interval training: will allow for rest breaks, which would be beneficial for a person who has not exercised for a long time.
- Circuit training: group exercise programme, which can help with motivation and also train the upper and lower body for muscular endurance, as well as aerobic endurance stations.
- Fartlek training: involves running at different speeds and on different terrain, which will be similar to the needs of the 5 km obstacle race.

Muscular endurance

- Resistance exercises using low weights (50% one rep max), high reps 10–15 and two to three sets.
- Fixed-resistance machines: good for a person who is new to exercise as less chance of injury from dropping the weights.
- Free weights: can progress onto these once the exercises have been practised for a period of time on fixed machines.
- Circuit training: using body weight, for example, press-ups, tricep dips, lunges, squats.

Equipment needed

- Suitable trainers for jogging.
- Sports clothing.
- Bicycle and helmet to cycle to work.
- Access to a leisure centre or group exercise class for circuit training.

Training principles to consider for Shelly

FITT

- **Frequency:** she needs to train at least three times a week to have an aerobic training effect.
- **Intensity:** aerobic endurance needs to be between 60 and 70% max heart rate, which is
  $$220 - 38 = 182$$
  $$182 \times 60/100 = 109 \text{ bpm}$$
  $$182 \times 70/100 = 127 \text{ bpm}.$$
- **Time:** at least 30 minutes for continuous aerobic endurance training.
- **Type of exercise:** she should ensure the training programme includes jogging and muscular endurance exercises that target the lower body and upper body.

Other principles

- **Specificity:** need to match training to needs of the sport.
- **Overload:** the training programme should show that there is continual overload over the course of the six weeks so that she is increasing the intensity and/or the length of the training session and/or number of sessions per week to have an overload effect.
- **Progression:** start slowly and build up. This is important for a person new to exercise as they may be at risk of getting injured if they try to do too much too soon. Shelly will need to increase the intensity of the exercise programme gradually over the six-week period.
- **Reversibility:** need to make sure training programme is realistic to prevent her taking too long a break or becoming injured, and to ensure that there is sufficient training to maintain the fitness gains she is making, to prevent reversibility.
- **Rest and recovery:** at least one rest day a week should be included in a training programme to allow the body to adapt to the training.
- **Adaptation:** the body responds to training by producing adaptations to the stresses of the exercise, which then allow it to deal more effectively with the exercise. Muscle tissue responds by getting bigger.

- **Variation:** need to ensure there is variation in exercise to prevent a person from getting bored.
- **Individual needs:** Shelly is unfit, aged 38 and does not have a history of enjoying exercise other than walking as part of a group. The programme needs to start gently and she may respond better to group exercise training.
- **Periodisation:** macrocyles, mesocyles and microcyles are ways to prepare a person so that their training is tailored so that they are specific even on a specific day – this is mainly related to elite athletes.

Pages 31–33: Lifestyle questionnaire

Prepare: Potential healthy swaps for those currently being eaten:

Crisps – homemade vegetable crisps, handful of nuts or carrot sticks.

Chocolate bar – piece of fruit.

Chocolate biscuits – yoghurt or fruit.

Crackers and cheese – carrot or celery sticks and cheese, or crackers and cottage cheese.

Prepare: The recommended alcohol limit is 14 units so Shelly is below the recommended weekly amount.

Prepare: Positive factors: low stress levels, below recommended alcohol intake, recommended amount of sleep.

Negative factors: smoking, lack of physical activity, non-balanced diet.

Prepare: Comparing data from notes with case study information can lead to compiling a table like this one:

Test	Result
Blood pressure	140/92 mmHg – hypertension
Resting heart rate	85 bpm – poor
Body mass index	25 – overweight
Waist-to-hip ratio	1.0 – high

All of these results raise health concerns.

Pages 34–36: Activity 1

Individual responses to interpret the **lifestyle factors and screening information** for Shelly. The following provides example points only, against which you can review your own work. The response should have a well-written and logical **structure**, looking at all aspects of the information you have been provided with.

You should include both **positive** and **negative** lifestyle factors in your response using the screening information, and each needs to be described comprehensively. The lifestyle factors that should be covered are sleep, diet, exercise, smoking, alcohol, stress and physical activity levels.

Positive lifestyle factors

- Stress: does not experience stress.
- Sleep: gets eight hours sleep per night.
- Alcohol: drinks considerably less than the recommended threshold of 14 units per week.

Negative lifestyle factors

- Smoking: smokes 20 cigarettes a day.
- Exercise: no physical activity.
- Diet: high in fat and sugar, low in fruit and vegetables.

You should take a detailed analytical approach to the lifestyle factors identified for the chosen individual, leading to an interpretation of the impact on their health and well-being. The interpretation should have specific relevance to the health and well-being of the individual.

Analysis of lifestyle factors

Positive lifestyle factors

- Low stress levels mean Shelly has a reduced risk of impacts on her immune system, heart disease, stroke, hypertension, angina, stomach ulcers, depression.
- Getting the recommended amount of sleep means Shelly's body has time to complete the phases it needs for muscle repair, memory consolidation, release of hormones regulating growth and appetite.
- Drinking less than the recommended threshold reduces Shelly's risk of many long-term health problems, including cancer, heart problems and mental health problems.

Negative lifestyle factors

- Smoking puts Shelly at increased risk of several cancers (for example, mouth, lung, liver, etc.), coronary heart disease, heart attack, stroke, vascular disease, COPD, worsening respiratory conditions and fertility problems. Smoking will also reduce the amount of oxygen that the body can take up as the alveoli are affected by smoking, so Shelly will find taking part in aerobic endurance exercises more difficult compared to a non-smoking person.
- Shelly currently takes part in no physical activity at all. Government recommendations are moderate activity five times a week, moderate activity of 150 minutes across the week and activity for strength twice a week. No exercise increases Shelly's risk of many serious health problems, including mental health problems, heart disease and obesity.
- Shelly's non-balanced diet increases her risk of many health conditions, and is likely to be delivering more calories than needed, which will cause weight gain and may cause constipation.

You also need to undertake a detailed analysis and interpretation of the health-monitoring test results for Shelly. The interpretation should be made specifically relevant to Shelly and her health and lifestyle. All four health-monitoring test results should be covered: resting heart rate, blood pressure, waist-to-hip ratio and BMI.

Test	Result	Rating
Blood pressure	140/92 mmHg	Stage 1 hypertension
Resting heart rate	85 bpm	Poor
Body mass index	25	Overweight
Waist-to-hip ratio	1.0	High

- Blood pressure: reading is high, falls into Stage 1 hypertension. Increased risk of heart attack, stroke, kidney disease, vascular dementia.
- Resting heart rate: poor – this is a very high result.
- BMI: overweight.
- Waist-to-hip ratio: 1.0. This is at top end of the scale. Increased risk of: hypertension, infertility, osteoarthritis, cardiovascular disease, type 2 diabetes, sleep apnoea.

Pages 37–39: Activity 2

Individual responses to **provide and justify lifestyle modification techniques** for Shelly. The following provides example points only, against which you can review your own work. The response should have a well-written and logical **structure,** looking at all aspects of the information you have been provided with.

Proposals of lifestyle modifications should be provided that clearly link to the lifestyle factor analysis you gave in Activity 1. The proposals given should demonstrate an understanding of significance, which includes the most important lifestyle modification techniques and why they are important.

Lifestyle modification techniques should demonstrate specific relevance to the individual's lifestyle and their requirements.

For Shelly, the key areas you should discuss are:

Smoking cessation. Stopping smoking is the most significant lifestyle change that Shelly could make to improve her health. She would significantly reduce the likelihood of several diseases. It would also help her in training for the 5 km obstacle race. By stopping smoking she could improve her energy levels and breathe better, both of which would help in increasing her exercise. Strategies to help Shelly stop smoking include:

- nicotine replacement therapy
- NHS smoking helplines
- NHS smoking services
- acupuncture
- Quit Kit support packs.

Note that at the same time as quitting smoking, the advice to improve diet and increase exercise could help to offset any potential risk of Shelly putting on weight, which could be a concern.

Increase exercise. Shelly currently undertakes no exercise. In order to be able to enjoy completing the 5 km obstacle race she needs to significantly improve her activity levels. As her reason for not taking part in sport or physical activity is because she doesn't enjoy it, a main focus of any training plan needs to be on finding activity that Shelly can enjoy or easily incorporate into her lifestyle. Some ideas could be:

- Suggesting non-competitive sports or group exercise classes. Shelly hasn't yet made friends in her new area. Team sports could enable her to make friends at the same time as increasing activity. Non-competitive sports would make it easier for a total beginner to join in.
- Using activity within her daily life. So walking or cycling to work some of the time, using her flexible working hours to take a long lunch break and go for a walk.
- Finding a local walking club as she used to enjoy this.

Weight loss. Shelly's BMI indicates that she falls into the overweight category, significantly increasing her risk of heart disease and diabetes, among other health problems. She also has a high waist-to-hip ratio. Both the BMI result and the waist-to-hip ratio indicate that Shelly is overweight and needs to reduce her calorie intake in order to lose weight. She should also increase her activity levels, which will help her lose excess body fat. Changing her diet and increasing activity levels should help to improve her body composition and therefore her BMI and waist-to-hip ratio, which will also help her to complete the obstacle race more effectively. Strategies could include:

- Using Eatwell Plate recommendations to improve nutrition.
- Eating smaller portion sizes.
- Swapping less healthy choices for healthier choices, such as swapping fried chips for oven-cooked chips, which reduces fat intake.
- Eating less processed foods and having healthier options, such as salmon, boiled potatoes and salad instead of chicken curry and fried rice.
- Cutting out biscuits and crisps, and replace with fruit and vegetables.
- Improving hydration levels by drinking fewer caffeinated drinks in the day, instead drinking water instead of tea or switching to decaffeinated or herbal teas.

Your answer should note any relevant barriers to change such as:

- Time: Shelly may not have much free time to train so consider where training can be blended into everyday life activities that will help prevent time being an issue and preventing her from training.
- Cost: Shelly will have to spend some money on buying equipment to go running and to cycle to work, however, she

could try to get a second-hand bike, which is much cheaper than a new one.

Pages 40–41: Activity 3

Individual responses to **provide and justify nutritional guidance** for Shelly. The following provides example points only, against which you can review your own work. The response should have a well-written and logical **structure** and should demonstrate specific relevance to the individual's requirements.

The recommended daily allowance of **calories** for Shelly should be stated. Quantities and sources of food for both **macronutrients** and **micronutrients** must be proposed as well as **hydration**. The proposed nutritional guidance should be justified, making it specifically relevant to Shelly's dietary requirements related to the food diary presented in the lifestyle questionnaire and the health-monitoring test results. Some key points are given below.

Calorie intake

- Energy intake for an adult woman should be around 2000 kcal per day.
- Shelly has a high BMI in the overweight category, which can be due to excess muscle tissue; however, as Shelly also has a high waist-to-hip ratio it indicates that she has a lot of excess body fat, which shows she is eating more calories than she needs.
- She needs to reduce her calorie intake to try to lose excess body weight.

Macronutrients

- Carbohydrate intake should be around 50–55% of the dietary intake.
  - Carbohydrates provide energy.
  - In Shelly's food diary, very few complex carbohydrates are eaten, just toast, chips, crisps and fried rice. Increasing complex carbohydrates (for example, brown or wholegrain toast, brown rice) would provide sustained energy.
- Protein intake should be around 15–20% of the dietary intake.
  - Protein is used for growth and repair of tissues.
  - Shelly's diet is relatively high in protein (on day 1 she ate sausages, bacon, pepperoni and fish. On day 2, she ate a burger and chicken). However, much of her protein intake is processed meat.
  - Guidance is to eat more non-processed protein (a chicken breast instead of a burger for example, as this is lower in saturated fat), and overall to reduce her protein intake to around 15–20% of her total diet.
- Fat intake should be around 30% of the dietary intake.
  - Fat is used for insulation and storage of vitamins.
  - Shelly's diet is currently high in saturated fat, such as fried eggs and fish and chips, salt from processed foods, such as pepperoni pizza, and these are also high in calories. Her diet is also low in wholegrain foods and low in fruit and vegetables as she only has one serving of vegetables, peas on day 1 and a piece of fruit on day 2, which means she is not eating the recommended five portions of fruit and vegetables per day.
  - Too much saturated fat can cause significant health issues. Women should consume no more than 20 g per day.
  - Guidance is to swap foods high in saturated fat for healthier choices. For example, boiling or poaching eggs instead of frying eggs, having boiled rice not fried, choosing salad instead of chips for some meals and using oven-baked chips. Snacks could be fruit or vegetables rather than biscuits and chocolate.

Micronutrients

Vitamins
- Vitamin A (fat-soluble): 0.6 mg needed per day for women.
  - Function: helps maintain good vision, healthy skin, hair and mucous membranes, is an antioxidant. Needed for proper bone and teeth development.
  - Sources: liver, mackerel, whole milk, green leafy vegetables, carrots, orange coloured fruits.
- Vitamin B:
  - Function: releases energy, aids in production of red blood cells.
  - Sources: lean meats, soya beans, leafy greens, fish, mushrooms, walnuts, eggs, cereal, wholegrains.
- Vitamin C: 40 mg per day needed.
  - Function: helps formation of collagen, is an antioxidant, helps in healing, fighting infections and helps the body to absorb iron.
  - Sources: citrus fruits, berries, green vegetables, peppers, tomatoes.
- Vitamin D:
  - Function: promotes strong bones and teeth.
  - Sources: mostly sunlight, some in fish, cheese, egg yolk, fortified cereals.

Minerals

- Calcium: 700 mg per day needed.
  - Function: builds strong bones and teeth, normal muscle function, blood clotting.
  - Sources: dairy foods, whole grains, fish bones, green leafy vegetables.
- Iron: 14.8 mg per day for women.
  - Function: needed for formation of haemoglobin in red blood cells, immune system, release of energy.
  - Sources: liver, meat, beans, nuts, dried fruits.

Hydration

- Shelly drinks around four cups of caffeinated drinks a day as tea and coffee both contain caffeine. Having too much caffeine can be harmful to health as it can prevent a person from getting to sleep at night, as well as causing anxiety and irritability. It can also lead to dehydration. Therefore, it would be better for Shelly to swap at least two cups of caffeinated drinks for decaffeinated drinks such as herbal tea, or decaffeinated tea or coffee.
- Shelly does drink two small bottles of water a day, but she needs to make sure she drinks the recommended daily amount of at least 2 litres per day. She would need to increase this amount when she takes part in her training programme as she will lose water through sweating when she is exercising, so she will need to ensure she increases her fluid intake and that she drinks water during and/or after exercising.

Pages 42–43: Activity 4

Individual responses to **propose and justify different training methods** that meet Shelly's training needs. The following provides example points only, against which you can review your own work. The response should have a well-written and logical **structure** and should demonstrate specific relevance to Shelly's training requirements.

You will need to state which methods of training would be most appropriate and why. In the lifestyle questionnaire, aerobic endurance and muscular endurance are noted as the key components of fitness that Shelly wants to improve upon. Some key points are given below.

Aerobic endurance

The 5 km obstacle race is likely to take more than 30 minutes, so increasing aerobic endurance will be needed to enable Shelly to achieve her goal.

- Continuous training: running/jogging at a steady pace for at least 30 minutes – can be carried out as part of her daily routine to travel to work. As 5 km is a long way to jog she

could start by cycling some of the distance, which is an aerobic activity and build up her aerobic endurance before starting to try to jog to work
- Interval training: as Shelly doesn't currently take part in any jogging type of exercise she would need to include rest periods where she jogs and walks rather than trying to jog for a long distance; therefore, interval training would be good so Shelly could jog for a period of time then have a rest period where she walks to recover and then jog again, repeating the process until she covers the set distance.
- Fartlek training: this may be more appropriate than continuous training as it involves running at different speeds and on different terrain, which will be similar to the needs of the 5 km obstacle race. This is something that Shelly would need to build up to; initially it would be best to start on flat surfaces and then build up to jogging up hills, as going uphill is at a higher intensity than on a flat surface.
- Circuit training: this involves stations with aerobic activities, usually performed in a group exercise class, which could also give Shelly the chance to meet people and help to add variety to her exercise programme.

Muscular endurance
- Improving upper body strength through resistance exercises will help Shelly when negotiating the obstacles.
- Resistance exercises using low weights (50% one rep max), high reps 10–15 and two to three sets.
- Fixed-resistance machines will be good for a person who is new to exercise as there is less chance of injury from dropping the weights, which is better for Shelly as she has not taken part in this type of training before
- Free weights would be useful for Shelly to progress onto once the exercises have been practised for a period of time on fixed machines.
- Circuit training sessions often have muscular-endurance-based stations that use body weight, such as press-ups, tricep dips, lunges, squats, all of which would be beneficial for Shelly.

Pages 44–46: Activity 5

Individual responses to **design weeks 1, 3 and 6 of a six-week training programme** for Shelly. The following provides example points only, against which you can review your own work. You will need to complete the tables provided for you.

For this activity you need to design a training programme that demonstrates specific relevance to all the fitness requirements for Shelly, which are aerobic and muscular endurance.

The training programme should also demonstrate a thorough understanding of the principles of fitness training, in the context of the individual's lifestyle or training requirements. The FITT principle must be applied in full detail to the programme, and you should be specific about the intensity of the activities.

Additional principles of fitness training must also be applied, such as specificity, overload, progression, reversibility, rest and recovery, adaptation, variation and individual needs.

Not all of the additional principles of fitness training need to be applied here but the programme must demonstrate a thorough understanding of these and that they have been taken into account when designing the three weeks of the six-week programme.

Include periodisation in your planning. Shelly needs to plan to make sure she is at the right level of fitness to complete the 5 km obstacle race. She has six weeks, which is her macrocycle, and each week of her programme is a mesocycle and each session a microcycle.

An example is given below:

Week 1

	Physical activity
Monday	Bus 3 km and walk 1 km to work – continuous training 60% max HR Bus 3 km and walk 1 km home from work – continuous training 60% max HR
Tuesday	Bus 3 km and speed-walk 1 km to work – continuous training 60% max HR Bus 3 km and speed-walk 1 km home from work – continuous training 60% max HR Evening Gym – 30-minute session – fixed-resistance machines hamstring curls, quad extensions, calf raises – 10–15 reps, two to three sets 55% one rep max Static stretching to finish
Wednesday	Bus 3 km and walk 1 km to work – continuous training 60% max HR Bus 3 km and walk 1 km home from work – continuous training 60% max HR
Thursday	Bus 3 km and walk 1 km to work – continuous training 60% max HR Bus 3 km and walk 1 km home from work – continuous training 60% max HR Evening Circuit training group session – body-weight resistance and aerobic stations
Friday	Bus 2.5 km and speed-walk 1.5 km to work – continuous training 60% max HR Bus 3 km and speed-walk 1 km home from work – continuous training 60% max HR
Saturday	Rest day
Sunday	30-minute jog and speed-walk interval training 60% max HR 10-minute static stretching

In week 1, this programme is focused on getting Shelly into exercise, introducing her to different types of activity and trying to make sure she enjoys the programme to increase her motivation

Week 3

	Physical activity
Monday	Bus 3 km and walk 1 km to work – continuous training 60% max HR Bus 3 km and walk 1 km home from work – continuous training 65% max HR 10-minute static stretching at home Evening 60 minutes Boot camp outdoor circuit session – aerobic exercise stations and muscular endurance body weight stations 65% max HR

Tuesday	Bus 2 km and jog and speed-walk 2 km to work – continuous training 60% max HR
	Bus 3 km and speed-walk 1 km home from work – continuous training 60% max HR
	Evening
	Gym – 30-minute session – fixed-resistance machines hamstring curls, quad extensions, calf raises – 12–15 reps, two to three sets
	60% one rep max
	Static stretching to finish
Wednesday	Cycle 4 km to work – continuous training 65% max HR
	Cycle 4 km home from work – continuous training 65% max HR
	Evening
	Gym – 30-minute session – fixed-resistance machines – chest press, bicep curls, tricep extensions, 12–15 reps two–three sets
	60% one rep max
	10 minutes static stretching to finish
Thursday	Bus 2 km and jog and speed-walk 2 km to work – continuous training 60% max HR
	Bus 3 km and speed-walk 1 km home from work – continuous training 60% max HR
	Evening
	60-minute circuit training group session – body weight resistance and aerobic stations 65% max HR
Friday	Cycle 4 km to work – continuous training 65% Max HR
	Cycle 4 km home from work – continuous training 65% max HR
	10 minutes static stretching after cycle home
Saturday	Rest day
Sunday	40-minute jog and speed-walk interval training 65% max HR
	10 minutes static stretching

In week 3, the programme shows progression by increasing aerobic training intensity to 65% max HR, as she is now cycling the whole distance to work and also introducing jogging to her journey into work as well as walking. Muscular endurance has increased the intensity and the number of reps.

Week 6

	Physical activity
Monday	Cycle 4 km to work – continuous training 70% max HR
	Cycle 4 km home from work – continuous training 70% max HR
	10 minutes static stretching after cycle home
	Evening
	60 minutes
	Boot-camp outdoor circuit session – aerobic exercise stations and muscular endurance body-weight stations
	70% max HR

Tuesday	Bus 1 km and jog 3 km to and from work – continuous training 70% max HR
	Evening
	Gym – 40-minute session – free weights machines – hamstring curls, quad extensions, calf raises – 15 reps, three sets
	60% one rep max
	Static stretching to finish
Wednesday	Cycle 4 km to work – continuous training 70% max HR
	Cycle 4 km home from work – continuous training 70% max HR
	Evening
	Gym – 40-minute session – free weights, chest press, bicep curls, tricep extensions, 15 reps, three sets
	60% one rep max
	10 minutes static stretching to finish
Thursday	Bus 1 km and jog 3 km to work – continuous training 70% max HR
	Bus 1 km and jog 3 km home from work – continuous training
	Evening
	60-minute circuit-training group session – body-weight resistance and aerobic stations 70% max HR
Friday	Cycle 4 km to work – continuous training 70% max HR
	Cycle 4 km home from work – continuous training 70% max HR
	10 minutes static stretching after cycle home
Saturday	Rest day
Sunday	40-minute cross-country jog 70% max HR
	10 minutes static stretching

Week 6 shows increased progression intensity of the training to 70% increase in max HR for aerobic training and increasing the number of reps and sets for muscular endurance training.

Pages 47–50: Activity 6

Individual responses to **justify the training programme** that you designed. The following provides example points only, against which you can review your own work. The response should have a well-written and logical **structure** and should show a thorough understanding of the principles of fitness training applied to the training programme.

The FITT principle must be justified in relation to the training programme and you should refer to the majority of the additional principles of fitness training such as specificity, overload, progression, reversibility, rest and recovery, adaptation, variation and individual needs in terms of the training programme that has been designed.

You will need to give a justification that demonstrates relevance to the design of the training programme and the training requirements of the individual. In your response you will need to justify the aims and objectives of the training programme for the chosen individual as well as any personal goals and resources required. Some key points related to the programme given in Activity 5 above are given. Yours will differ according to the activities you included.

Shelly's goals are to increase aerobic and muscular endurance. In order to do this, the programme has been designed using FITT and other principles of training. Shelly currently undertakes no physical activity so the programme is designed to give progression from lower to higher rates of activity. Shelly does not enjoy sport or physical activity so the plan uses activities that are likely to be more enjoyable and therefore give Shelly more motivation to continue. Some key points are below.

The FITT principles have been applied in designing this training programme:

- **Frequency:** training takes place six times a week.
- **Intensity:** intensity is sufficient to have an aerobic training effect for aerobic endurance as the maximum percentage heart rate is in the aerobic training zone. Muscular endurance exercises show an increase in one rep max intensity as the weeks progress.
- **Time:** time spent training from week 1 to week 6 increases from distance covered in the cycling and walking to work as well as longer distances on cross-country jogging and progressively increasing the time spent in the gym.
- **Type:** the activities cycling, walking and jogging are all to increase aerobic fitness and the gym and circuit training help to train muscular endurance.

Other principles of training also considered:

- **Specificity:** the training is specific to completing an obstacle course, which requires jogging and the ability to get over obstacles, so cardiovascular fitness and muscular endurance need to be trained.
- **Overload:** provided by increasing the intensity and time in aerobic training. For muscular endurance, intensity of the one rep max is increased over the six weeks for the weight lifted.
- **Progression:** each week the time spent training increases and the intensity gradually increases from 60–80% max HR for aerobic fitness and from 55% 1 rep max to 60% one rep max for muscular endurance training.
- **Reversibility:** this should not occur as there are sufficient training sessions to prevent it.
- **Rest and recovery:** there is always one day a week that is a rest day to allow the muscles to repair and adapt from the training.
- **Adaptation:** the aerobic energy systems and cardiorespiratory systems should have adapted to the training and be able to cope with longer exercise periods and at higher intensity. The muscles that are trained by the gym exercises should also adapt to the training so that they are stronger and more able to cope with lifting heavier loads.
- **Variation:** the circuit training session can be varied from week to week with different types of stations to maintain motivation. Cross-country training can take place over different routes to maintain interest rather than just going round a running track.
- **Individual needs:** a lot of the training takes place during the journey to and from work, which helps Shelly fit the training into her daily routine as she works long hours.

Resources:

- Bicycle and helmet to cycle to and from work.
- Suitable exercise clothing.
- Access to a gym with fixed-resistance machines.
- Access to a circuit group exercise class.
- Cross-country running requires access to outdoor running areas such as pavements, cross-country routes or a running track.

Practice assessment 3

Pages 51–55: Research and notes

Page 51: Revision task

Prepare: You may underline, highlight or circle the following parts of the case study:

Case study

Raj is 27 years old and works eight hours a day as a personal trainer. His work involves visiting people's homes and delivering personal training sessions for each client. Sometimes the sessions he runs require him to take part in a lot of physical activity, such as going on a run with a client. Other times he is mainly involved with checking the client's exercise technique, such as ensuring they are lifting weights correctly, which does not require a great deal of exertion from him.

When he finishes a personal training session with one client, he cycles to his next client's house. The distances he cycles range from 0.5 km to 5 km and he usually cycles 15 km per day.

He usually has five clients booked per day, with each session lasting at least an hour.

Raj used to take part in weightlifting. His local area is hosting a weightlifting competition and he has decided he would like to get back into the sport and enter this competition.

Page 52: Research notes on lifestyle factors and screening information

Normative health data for 27-year-old male
BMI

- Underweight: <18.5 kg/m^2
- Normal: 18.5–24.9 kg/m^2
- Overweight: 25–29.9 kg/m^2
- Obese: 30–39.9 kg/m^2
- Very obese: >40 kg/m^2

High BMI increased risks: hypertension, osteoarthritis, sleep apnoea, type 2 diabetes, cardiovascular disease.

Low BMI increased risks: osteoporosis, anaemia.

Waist-to-hip ratio (men)

- Excellent: <0.85
- Good: 0.85–0.90
- Average: 0.90–0.95
- High: >0.95

Above 1.0 indicates too much weight around the middle, increasing risk of diabetes, stroke and heart disease.

Blood pressure

- Low: 70–90 mmHg (systolic)/40–60 mmHg (diastolic)
- Ideal: 90–120 mmHg (systolic)/60–80 mmHg (diastolic)
- Pre-high blood pressure: 120–140 mmHg (systolic)/80–90 mmHg (diastolic)
- High blood pressure: >140 mmHg (systolic)/>90 mmHg (diastolic)

High blood pressure increased risks: heart attack, stroke, kidney disease and vascular dementia.

There are different sources with slightly differing values for blood pressure. As long as the source that you have used is a reliable source, such as a national health web page or an endorsed textbook, then the values you use will be acceptable in your exam.

Resting heart rate for men aged 26–35

Athlete	49–54
Excellent	55–61
Good	62–65
Above average	66–70
Average	71–74
Below average	75–81
Poor	82+

Resting heart rate (RHR) improves with fitness.

Government/health recommendations

- Maximum of 14 units of alcohol per week for a man.
  - Risks if drinking more than this: mouth, throat and/or breast cancer, stroke, heart disease, liver disease, brain damage, nervous system damage.
  - 1 pint beer = 2 units, 1 glass wine = 2.5 units, 1 measured spirits = 1 unit.
- No smoking. Risks of smoking: lung and other cancers, chronic obstructive pulmonary disease (COPD), stroke, heart disease.
- 10 000 steps per day or 30 minutes of moderate intensity exercise 5 days per week.
- Seven to eight hours of sleep per night and regular sleeping patterns. Poor sleep can cause: low immune system, heart disease, diabetes, poor mental health, stress, memory problems.

Demands of personal trainer as occupation

- High levels of physical activity.
- Potentially stressful coaching others.
- Working hours may be unpredictable, with early starts/late finishes. Could make it tricky to fit in training sessions/classes on a regular basis.

Page 53: Research notes on nutritional requirements for 27-year-old male

- Energy intake: 2500–3500 kcal a day.

> Raj's energy needs are likely to be higher than this due to his very active lifestyle, as he takes part in exercise classes with his clients up to five times a day and cycles to each client's house. His energy requirements are therefore going to be much more than 2500 kcal per day. He may need to consume 3500 kcal or more.

- Caffeine: guidelines are a maximum of up to four cups per day.

Macronutrients

- Carbohydrate: 50–60% of the diet. Raj takes part in a lot of physical activity so will need high levels of carbohydrates to provide energy for this physical activity.
  - Function: provides an energy source for sport. More active individuals may need up to 70% of their diet as complex carbohydrates to replace depleted glycogen stores.
  - Sources: sugar, fruit, bread, rice, pasta.
- Fat: 20–35% of diet. This will be needed at the lower percentage of recommended daily allowance (RDA) as Raj will need more protein in his diet.
  - Function: provides energy for low-intensity exercise, insulates the body, protects internal organs.
  - Sources: oils, dairy, butter, fatty meat, biscuits.
  - Men should consume no more than 30 g saturated fat per day.
- Protein: 12–20% is the RDA for an average person. As Raj wants to increase his muscle mass a diet high in protein is required, so around 20% of calorie intake should come from protein.
  - Function: growth and repair.
  - Sources: meat, fish, eggs, cheese, milk, beans.
  - An average man should consume no more than 55 g protein per day; however, as Raj wants to increase his muscle mass he may benefit from eating at least 55g per day.

> Someone wanting to increase their strength will need to increase their protein intake as protein is necessary for muscle growth and repair. The more muscle mass a person has the stronger they are.

Micronutrients
Vitamins

- Vitamin A (fat-soluble): 0.7 mg needed per day for men.
  - Function: helps maintain good vision, healthy skin, hair and mucous membranes, is an antioxidant. Needed for proper bone and teeth development.
  - Sources: liver, mackerel, whole milk, green leafy vegetables, carrots, orange coloured fruits.
- Vitamin B
  - Function: releases energy, aids in production of red blood cells.
  - Sources: lean meats, soya beans, leafy greens, fish, mushrooms, walnuts, eggs, cereal, wholegrains.
- Vitamin C: 40 mg per day needed.
  - Function: formation of collagen, an antioxidant, helps in healing, fighting infections and helps the body to absorb iron.
  - Sources: citrus fruits, berries, green vegetables, peppers, tomatoes.
- Vitamin D:
  - Function: promotes strong bones and teeth.
  - Sources: mostly sunlight, some in fish, cheese, egg yolk, fortified cereals.

Minerals

- Calcium: 700 mg per day needed.
  - Function: builds strong bones and teeth, normal muscle function, blood clotting.
  - Sources: dairy foods, whole grains, fish bones, green leafy vegetables.
- Iron: 8.7 mg per day for men needed.
  - Function: helps in formation of haemoglobin in red blood cells, strengthens immune system, releases energy.
  - Sources: liver, meat, beans, nuts, dried fruits.

Hydration

- 1.5–2 litres (six to eight cups) per day for sedentary adult. As Raj is active, likely to require more than this so aim for at least 2.5–3 litres.
- Dehydration problems: impaired strength, power and aerobic capacity.
- Needed for transporting nutrients, regulating temperature, digestive system.
- Fluid needed before, during and after event.
- As Raj is out and about between clients' houses, he will need to think about how to maintain hydration through the day, especially when he is active.
- Some fluid intake comes from fruit and vegetables.

Nutrition

- **Fruits and vegetables:** should make up a third of the food eaten each day. At least five portions should be eaten each day. Good sources of vitamins and minerals.
- **Starchy carbohydrates (potatoes, bread, rice, pasta):** should make up just over a third of the food eaten. High-fibre, wholegrain varieties should be eaten where possible to provide sustained energy release throughout the day, which a very active person needs.
- **Milk and dairy products:** around three servings per day of milk, cheese, yoghurt, etc. Low-fat versions are preferable, for example, skimmed milk rather than full fat.
- **Beans, pulses, fish, eggs, meat and other protein:** two portions per day at least for a person wanting to build muscle mass. Meat and meat products plus vegetarian meat substitutes such as Quorn or tofu. Protein supplements could also be consumed to ensure Raj is eating sufficient protein.
- **Fats, oils and sweets:** eat only small quantities of foods from this group. This group includes foods containing high quantities of fats and oils, for example, butter, margarine, olive oil, cakes, biscuits, pastries, ice cream, cream and fried foods such as chips, burgers, etc., and foods containing high quantities of sugar, such as fizzy drinks (not diet drinks), sweets, cakes, puddings, chocolate and jam.
- **Salt:** salt is needed to maintain fluid balance, but too much salt can lead to high blood pressure and heart disease. High salt

levels are often found in processed foods, such as crisps, pre-prepared meals. An adult should eat no more than 6 g per day.

Pages 54–55: Research notes on training methods and designing a training programme

- Fitness components for weightlifting: strength (physical) and power (skill: strength × speed)
- **Physical fitness:**
  Muscular strength training
  Resistance exercises are required to increase strength.
  High weights low reps.
  Pyramid sets.

  Power training
  To increase power, plyometrics can be used.
  Both upper body and lower body will need to be trained.
  Lunges, squats, medicine ball throws, press-ups on and off blocks.

  Core stability
  A range of different exercises can be used:
  Plank, press-ups, crunches – these could be performed at the end of a muscular training or power training session just before the cool down.
  He could go to Pilates as a group exercise.

Equipment needed

- Free weights help to develop strength and also engage the fixator and synergist muscles to control the lifting of the weights, which is beneficial for balanced strength gains.
- A spotter is needed for free weights to ensure the health and safety of the person lifting the weights so that they do not drop them on themselves when they are nearing the end of their set and their muscles are fatigued, such as in a bench press.
- Fixed weights are useful for a person new to weight training as they provide a specific movement pattern to follow and do not require the same level of involvement in synergists and fixators as free weights.
- A spotter is not usually needed when using fixed-resistance machines as the person can return the weight to the set position quite easily once the set is completed.

Training principles to consider for Raj

SMARTER objectives should be included when planning the training programme.

FITT:

- **Frequency:** weight training should be carried out regularly throughout the week with the muscle groups trained on alternating days to give the muscles time to recover and adapt. Two days a week could focus on the upper body and two days a week could focus on the lower body. Plyometric training could be carried out one day per week and core stability training could be integrated into the weight-training workouts. Raj will also need to be flexible with his own training programme, bearing in mind the active sessions he has with his clients.
- **Intensity:** workload is measure of intensity for strength training. Made up of weight, number of reps and number of sets. 2–4-min rests between sets. Higher intensity = more rest, lower intensity = less rest. To avoid fatigue, work large muscle groups first, then smaller. Leave abdominals until last (act as stabiliser for other muscle groups).
- **Time:** sessions no more than 45–60 minutes; if intense could be 20–30 minutes.
- **Type** of exercise: includes resistance machines, free weights, medicine balls, circuit training, core stability training.

Other:

- **Specificity:** the main aim is to increase strength, so the training needs to be specific to increase muscular strength.
- **Overload:** the muscles must be overloaded sufficiently to cause microtears to stimulate muscle growth. Raj needs to consider what he can lift already and try to increase this.
- **Progression:** over the six-week period there should be a gradual increase in weights used in order to continue to overload the muscle and promote muscle growth.
- **Reversibility:** if training is not carried out at regular intervals the muscle tissue will no longer increase in size, and strength will no longer increase.
- **Rest and recovery:** muscles need time to repair after a training session so it is a good idea to train different muscle groups on different days to give the worked muscle group time to rest.
- **Adaptation:** adaptation occurs during the rest and recovery stages where the microtears produced from resistance-training repair, which leads to the muscle tissue getting bigger and adapting to cope with the stress from resistance training.
- **Variation:** lifting weights over a six-week period can get a bit boring so it is important to try to vary the training programme where possible by adding in some different types of training methods. It would also be a good idea to add some form of flexibility training to help elongate the muscles after heavy workouts as they can remain contracted after strength training if not fully stretched out afterwards. Raj does get quite a bit of variety already, given the different sessions he runs with his clients.
- **Individual needs:** the person is an experienced exercise professional who has lifted weights before so the training programme needs to be sufficiently challenging. He does not require much guidance or support when taking part in the exercise programme.
- **Periodisation:** as Raj has a specific date to be ready for the competition, periodisation is important. The macrocycle is what happens over a 1- to 4-year cycle, which is too long for Raj to be concerned with as the competition is likely to occur before then. This training programme forms part of a mesocycle and he would have a ratio of a six-week training programme followed by a week of rest as he is an experienced trainer. A microcycle usually lasts one week; the training programme will show a week's microcycle for weeks 1, 3 and 6 of the training programme, which is the mesocycle.

Prepare: An objective Raj could set would be to be able to organise at least one client a day to have their training session at the gym, which would then allow Raj to train in the gym before or after the client's session.

A personal goal could be to ensure he makes time to go to one yoga class a week.

Raj would need to follow the FITT principles and additional principles of training in order to improve his strength and power.

Page 56–58: Lifestyle questionnaire

Prepare: Foods high in carbohydrates in Raj's nutritional programme include:

- porridge
- pasta
- mashed potatoes
- banana
- flapjack
- muesli
- boiled rice
- brown toast
- jam
- smoothie.

He also has energy gels, a food supplement high in carbohydrates.

This shows that Raj is eating the right amount of carbohydrates on the whole to meet the recommended daily amount of 50% intake.

Food high in protein in Raj's nutritional programme include:

- salmon
- chicken fillet
- mixed nuts.

From this it is clear that he is not eating enough protein to meet the recommended daily amount, which is 55 g per day, or two portions of protein a day.

Prepare: Raj should be drinking at least 2–2.5 litres of fluid a day; however, his nutritional status shows he only drinks 1 litre of water a day, which is not enough to keep him fully hydrated. This is because he is physically active and will lose water through sweat. He does eat a lot of fruit and vegetables that contain some water, as does a smoothie, but he still needs to increase his daily water intake to be fully hydrated. Dehydration has a negative impact on sports performance as well as on health so it is important that he does increase his fluid intake.

Prepare: Comparing alcohol intake for Raj with guidelines shows that Raj drinks five units of alcohol in a typical week. This is safely less than the recommendation of 14 units maximum a week.

Prepare: Looking at positive and negative lifestyle factors for Raj you could note the following.

Positive: safe alcohol intake; does not smoke.

Negative: feels stress in managing time and energy; sleeps for slightly under recommended seven to eight hours a night. During this time, muscle repair will take place after having completed weight training so it is very important that he has sufficient sleep. Stress and lack of sleep can lead to hypertension, angina, stroke, heart attack, stomach ulcers, depression and overeating.

Prepare: Some things that could help Raj meet his goals include: He could go to bed earlier each night to ensure he has at least eight hours sleep each night.

He could also only have one cup of coffee per day, which will help him to get to sleep sooner as caffeine is a stimulant and can stop people getting to sleep.

Pages 59–61: Activity 1

Individual responses to interpret the **lifestyle factors and screening information** for Raj. The following provides example points only, against which you can review your own work. The response should have a well-written and logical **structure,** looking at all aspects of the information you have been provided with.

You should include both **positive** and **negative** lifestyle factors in your response, using the screening information, and each needs to be described comprehensively. The lifestyle factors that should be covered are sleep, diet, exercise, smoking, alcohol, stress and physical activity levels.

Positive lifestyle factors

- Physical activity levels – Raj has an active job (active for around three hours a day), cycles between clients and weight trains for around one hour a day.
- Diet – balanced diet.
- Smoking – does not smoke.
- Alcohol – below guidelines.

Negative lifestyle factors

- Stress – high stress levels from work.
- Sleep – only six hours sleep a night, which is less than recommended (seven to eight hours per night).

You should give a detailed analysis of the lifestyle factors identified for the chosen individual, leading to an interpretation of their impact on their health and well-being. The interpretation should have specific relevance to the health and well-being of the individual.

Analysis of lifestyle factors
Positive lifestyle factors

- Physical activity: high levels of physical activity will help to strengthen bones. Also improve posture, reduce risk of coronary heart disease (CHD), cancer and type 2 diabetes. In addition, they will relieve stress and reduce risk or depression.
- Diet: healthy food options selected, lots of fruit and vegetables, low-fat diet – reduced risk of CHD.
- Alcohol intake: low levels of alcohol intake reduce risk of liver cirrhosis, stroke, hypertension and depression.

Negative lifestyle factors

- Diet: the nutritional programme shows that Raj does not eat a great deal and may not be taking in sufficient calories for the amount of energy he uses on a daily basis as he is very active.
- Stress: high levels of stress can lead to hypertension, angina, stroke, heart attack, stomach ulcer, and depression.
- Sleep: limited sleep can lead to depression and overeating.

You also need to undertake a detailed analytical approach and interpretation of the health-monitoring test results for Raj. The interpretation should be made specifically relevant to Raj and his health and lifestyle. All four health-monitoring test results should be covered: resting heart rate, blood pressure, waist-to-hip ratio and BMI.

Test	Result	Rating
Blood pressure	120/80 mmHg	Normal
Resting heart rate	56 bpm	Excellent
Body mass index	26	Overweight
Waist-to-hip ratio	0.78	Excellent

- Resting heart rate is low which shows he has high levels of aerobic endurance. This also means he has reduced risk of CHD and stroke.
- Low waist-to-hip ratio, so low levels of body fat around the internal organs – reduced risk of CHD. This also confirms that the BMI value is incorrect as he must have a high muscle mass rather than high fat mass to account for the overweight category rating from the BMI test result.
- BMI score is overweight; however, as a body builder, given his excellent waist-to-hip ratio, it is likely the high BMI rating is caused by excess muscle mass rather than excess fat.
- Blood pressure is rated at normal so less chance of stroke, CHD and heart attack.

Pages 62–64: Activity 2

Individual responses to **provide and justify lifestyle modification techniques** for Raj. The following provides example points only, against which you can review your own work. The response should have a well-written and logical **structure,** looking at all aspects of the information you have been provided with.

Proposals of lifestyle modifications should be provided that systematically link to the lifestyle factor analysis you gave in Activity 1. The proposals given should demonstrate an understanding of significance, which includes the most important lifestyle modification technique and why it should be undertaken.

Lifestyle modification techniques should demonstrate specific relevance to the individual's lifestyle and their requirements.

For Raj, the key areas you should discuss are:

Stress management techniques. Raj has identified that he experiences stress on a daily basis. Stress can lead to a range of chronic diseases, such as high blood pressure, angina, stroke, heart attack, stomach ulcers and depression. Always having to worry about being on time for clients is stressful and will occur throughout the day as Raj sees a number of clients each day. This stress can have a significant impact on an individual in relation to their health, as well as affecting their ability to go to sleep and stay asleep. Reducing his stress levels should help address the other lifestyle factors identified below. Strategies to reduce stress could include:

- relaxation classes such as yoga (this could also help with sleep and core stability as well as flexibility)
- breathing techniques – could be carried out in lunch break or when travelling to the next client to cope with the stress experienced between clients
- investigating what classes are provided at the gym where he carries out weight training to help with stress management as if it is onsite it will be easier to get to after working out
- try to move some clients so that their personal training session takes place at the gym so he doesn't have the stress of worrying about getting to the next client on time as they will be located in the same place.

Increase sleep. Lack of sleep could be causing health problems. Raj has a physically tiring job and is weight training an hour a day. Additional sleep could help with recovery as well as stress levels (although improving stress levels may also help with sleeping better). Strategies could include:

- reduce caffeine intake by, for example, drinking decaffeinated tea
- try to go to bed earlier to aim for seven to eight hours sleep a night
- try to take part in some form of relaxation technique, such as breathing techniques, while having a hot bath before going to sleep.

Improving nutrition. Raj has quite a low protein intake, which is not sufficient for a person who needs to increase their muscle strength. Strategies could include:

- Making a packed lunch that contains at least one portion of protein such as fish or chicken to help his muscles and body tissues grow and repair. He should also include some fruit and vegetables to supply fibre to aid digestion and excretion of food and avoid constipation, as well as supply vitamins. This would be very important for Raj as he is very physically active, which can stress the immune system.
- Including more starchy food, such as brown bread, to supply sustained energy to help ensure Raj has enough energy for the work he does as a personal trainer.
- If he finds it difficult to eat a full lunch as he won't have time to digest the food properly before he has to take part in physical activity again, he could have protein supplements, such as protein shakes, which are very easy to make and transport when at work, as well as quick and easy to consume. As they are in liquid format they will also be easier to digest.
- Increasing his water intake as currently he does not drink enough water to remain fully hydrated, which is harmful to his health as well as physical activity performance.

Pages 65–66: Activity 3

Individual responses to **provide and justify nutritional guidance** for Raj. The following provides example points only, against which you can review your own work. The response should have a well-written and logical **structure** and should demonstrate specific relevance to the individual's requirements.

The recommended daily allowance of **calories** for the individual should be stated and the fact that Raj has an active job role should be taken into consideration here. Quantities and sources of food for both **macronutrients** and **micronutrients** must be proposed, as well as **hydration**. The proposed nutritional guidance should be justified, making it specifically relevant to the individual's dietary requirements related to the food diary presented in the lifestyle questionnaire and the health-monitoring test results. Some key points are given below.

Calorie intake

- Energy intake for an adult man should be around 2500 kcal per day.
- His active lifestyle means that the average daily number of calories of 2500 kcal per day may not be sufficient to meet the additional energy demands of Raj's job as a personal trainer. He will therefore need to consume more calories in order to maintain energy levels throughout the day, as well as be able to take part in the planned training programme.

Macronutrients

- Carbohydrate intake should be around 50–55% of the dietary intake.
  - He has quite a high carbohydrate intake as he eats foods high in carbohydrates for every meal, for example, porridge is high in complex carbohydrates, as is pasta; this means they release energy slowly, which is good for Raj as he is active all day.
  - He has snacks that are high in carbohydrates, but he may need more energy for all the exercise he does on a daily basis and as carbohydrates provide most of the fuel for this he could increase his carbohydrate intake. He could drink carbohydrate sports drinks for example, which will increase his fluid intake, as well as provide a source of fuel.
- Protein intake should be around 20% of the dietary intake. As a strength athlete who wants to gain muscle mass, he should be eating the higher end of the 15–20% protein intake that is recommended for health and well-being.
  - Protein is used for growth and repair of tissues; it is therefore needed for repair of the muscle fibres that are broken down in training and for muscle hypertrophy to occur.
  - Current intake suggests he does not have sufficient protein intake as he only eats salmon and chicken on day 1, which both contain protein, and some nuts, which also contain protein. However, on day 2 he does not have any food sources that are high in protein as he does not eat any meat or dairy, which are foods that are high in protein.
  - He should try to eat some protein for every meal, such as eggs for breakfast (poached eggs on toast or scrambled eggs), and he should have a portion of protein for lunch, such as cheese or meat, and again, another portion of protein for dinner, such as chicken or fish. He could also consume protein shakes as snacks as a supplement to increase his protein intake.
- Fat intake should be around 30% of the dietary intake.
  - Fat is used for insulation and storage of vitamins.
  - His fat intake is very low as he eats very few foods that contain fat, just a flapjack on both days, and there are low levels of fat in other foods such as mashed potatoes. Salmon also contains fats that are required for good health.
  - He should increase his fat intake in order to increase his calorie intake, for example, he could snack on avocado or add it to his salad – avocado is high in good fats.

Micronutrients
Vitamins:

- Raj eats at least five servings of fruit and vegetables a day, which indicates he should be eating enough of the following vitamins:
  - Vitamin A – found in carrots for dinner on day 1.
  - Vitamin B – found in chicken.

o Vitamin C – found in blueberries, which he has on his porridge and in the fruits used for the smoothies (oranges, kiwis).
o Vitamin D – found in salmon.

He is not eating quite the right types of foods to ensure he is eating the right amount of minerals.

- Iron – this is found in nuts, but he only eats a small bag of nuts on day 1. He could eat red meat or beans to increase his iron intake. As he is so active he will need iron to help to develop red blood cells for aerobic exercise.
- Calcium – this is found in dairy foods, but he only eats porridge and muesli for breakfast, which are probably both made with milk. Apart from that he eats no other dairy foods. He should increase his calcium uptake, for example by having cheese, instead of jam, on toast as a snack and he could also eat a yoghurt, which is easy to carry in a packed lunch to eat between visiting clients.

Hydration

- Raj drinks two strong coffees a day. Having too much caffeine can be harmful to health as it can prevent a person from getting to sleep at night, and as well as causing anxiety and irritability, it can also lead to dehydration. Therefore, it would be better for Raj to swap one strong coffee to a decaffeinated drink such as herbal tea or decaffeinated tea or coffee.
- Raj only drinks 1 litre of water a day, which is not enough. He should be drinking more than the recommended amount for an average adult male, which is 1.5–2 litres per day. He should be drinking at least 2 litres per day. He could also drink sports drinks, such as isotonic sports drinks, to increase the absorption of fluids as they contain electrolytes and carbohydrates, which enable faster absorption compared to water alone. They will also provide additional energy to support Raj through his active daily tasks.

Pages 67–68: Activity 4

Individual responses to **propose and justify different training methods** that meet Raj's training needs. The following provides example points only, against which you can review your own work. The response should have a well-written and logical **structure** and should demonstrate specific relevance to Raj's training requirements.

You will need to state which methods of training would be most appropriate and why. In the lifestyle questionnaire, strength and core stability are the key components of fitness that Raj wants to improve upon. Some key points are given below.

Muscular strength
The main method to increase strength is to take part in resistance training with high loads and low reps. The training needs to be sufficient to overload the muscle fibres and cause microtears, which stimulate the process of hypertrophy.

Possible training could include:
- free weights
- fixed-resistance machines
- pyramid sets.

Free weights help to develop strength and also engage the fixator and synergist muscles to control the lifting of the weights, which is beneficial for balanced strength gains. A spotter is needed for free weights to ensure the health and safety of the person lifting the weights so that they do not drop them on themselves when they are nearing the end of their set and their muscles are fatigued, such as in a bench press.

Fixed weights are useful for a person new to weight training as they provide a specific movement pattern to follow and do not require

the same level of involvement in synergists and fixators as free weights.

A spotter is not usually needed when using fixed-resistance machines as the person can return the weight to the set position quite easily once the set is completed.

Core stability
The core muscles consist of the abdominals, erector spinae, pelvic floor muscles and transversus abdominis. Core stability is very important for weightlifting in order to prevent damage to the back when lifting heavy weights. To train core stability a number of different methods can be used, including gym-based exercises and group-based exercise classes. Possible training methods could include:
- Pilates
- yoga
- gym-based exercises, including plank, bridge, v-sit, power training.

Power
Training could include plyometrics. This process involves rebounding to fully stretch the muscle in an eccentric contraction followed by a very quick concentric contraction.

Equipment required:
- ladders
- cones
- jump ropes
- medicine ball
- hurdles
- benches
- fixed weights
- free weights – dumb-bells, barbells and weights.

Pages 69–71: Activity 5

Individual responses to **design weeks 1, 3 and 6 of a six-week training programme** for Raj. The following provides example points only, against which you can review your own work. You will need to complete the tables provided for you.

For this activity you need to design a training programme that demonstrates specific relevance to all Raj's fitness requirements, which are strength and core stability.

The training programme should also demonstrate a thorough understanding of the principles of fitness training, in the context of the individual's lifestyle or training requirements. The FITT principle must be applied in full detail to the programme, and you should be specific about the intensity of the activities.

The training programme should have a range of activities to ensure there is variety in the programme to maintain interest levels and avoid boredom. There is a progressive increase in intensity of how hard Raj should work over the six-week period as the body will adapt to the training and will be able to cope with higher levels of stress. Increases in exercise intensity are shown by % rep max for resistance training. There will also need to be progressive increases in intensity in order to overload the body systems so that they adapt to the training. Each training session includes types of training that are specific to train the required components of fitness identified to improve weightlifting performance.

Additional principles of fitness training must also be applied, such as specificity, overload, progression, reversibility, rest and recovery, adaptation, variation, periodisation and individual needs.

Not all of the additional principles of fitness training need to be applied here but the programme must demonstrate a thorough understanding of these and that they have been taken into account when designing the three weeks of the six-week programme.

An example is given below:

Week 1

	Physical activity
Monday	Fixed-weight resistance exercises – legs, back and buttocks 75% one rep max – 60 minutes
Tuesday	Rest day
Wednesday	Fixed-weight resistance exercises – 60 minutes – arms, chest, shoulders 75% one rep max
Thursday	Plyometrics – 30 minutes Pilates – 30 minutes
Friday	Fixed-weight resistance exercises – legs, back and buttocks 75% one rep max – 60 minutes Core stability exercises – 10 minutes
Saturday	Rest day
Sunday	Fixed-weight resistance exercises – 60 minutes – arms, chest, shoulders 75% one rep max

Raj has two rest days in his training programme to take into account the fact he is very physically active as part of his daily work as a personal trainer and he will also need more rest for his body to adapt to the training. One day will need to be a total rest day, which is Saturday, to ensure his body has time to adapt. The Tuesday rest day will be a rest day from weight training but not from his working life as a personal trainer. This programme starts with fixed-resistance weights to help to support Raj as he gets back into weight training as he hasn't done it for a while. This is a safer approach than using free weights, as the machines will only allow the weights to be lifted in a set manner to ensure the movement pattern is correct.

Week 3

	Physical activity
Monday	Free-weight resistance exercises – 60 minutes – legs, back and buttocks 80% one rep max Plyometrics upper body exercise – 10 minutes
Tuesday	Yoga group exercise class – 60 minutes
Wednesday	Free-weight resistance exercises – 60 minutes – arms, chest, shoulders 80% one rep max
Thursday	Plyometric upper and lower body Pilates for core stability – 70 minutes
Friday	Free-weight resistance exercises – 60 minutes – legs, back and buttocks 80% one rep max
Saturday	Free-weight resistance exercises – arms, chest, shoulders 80% one rep max Plyometrics – lower body Core stability exercises – 75 minutes
Sunday	Rest day

Free weights have been introduced as these will also engage synergist and fixator muscles in the lifting process and replicate the free-weight competition that Raj is entering. The intensity of the weight training has increased in order to ensure the muscles are overloaded to produce micro tears to stimulate muscle hypertrophy. Also added in is an increased number of plyometric exercise days as the body is adapting to the increased exercise demands. Also, Pilates has been introduced to help to improve core stability as well as add variation.

Week 6

	Physical activity
Monday	Free-weight resistance exercises – legs, back and buttocks 85% one rep max core stability – 70 minutes Plyometrics – lower body – 10 minutes
Tuesday	Yoga group exercise class – 60 minutes
Wednesday	Free-weight resistance exercises – arms, chest, shoulders 85% one rep max 60 minutes
Thursday	Plyometric – upper and lower body Pilates for core stability – 80 minutes
Friday	Free-weight resistance exercises – 60 minutes – legs, back and buttocks 85% one rep max
Saturday	Free-weight resistance exercises – arms, chest, shoulder – 85% one rep max Core stability exercises – 80 minutes Plyometrics – lower body – 10 minutes
Sunday	Rest day

In week 6, there is an increased intensity of weights to 85% to provide continued overload to muscles. More time is also spent on plyometrics and core stability

Pages 72–75: Activity 6

Individual responses to **justify the training programme** that you designed. The following provides example points only, against which you can review your own work. The response should have a well-written and logical **structure** and should show a thorough understanding of the principles of fitness training applied to the training programme.

The FITT principle must be justified in relation to the training programme and you should refer to the majority of the additional principles of fitness training, such as specificity, overload, progression, reversibility, rest and recovery, adaptation, variation and individual needs in terms of the training programme that has been designed.

You will need to give a justification that demonstrates relevance to the design of the training programme and the training requirements of the individual. In your response you will need to justify the aims and objectives of the training programme for the chosen individual, as well as any personal goals and resources required. Some key points related to the programme given in Activity 5 above are given. Your responses will differ according to the activities you included.

Raj's goals are to increase strength and core stability to improve his weightlifting performance, which requires muscular strength, core stability and power. In order to do this, the programme has been designed using FITT and other training principles. He is already very fit, with a normal blood pressure and resting heart rate, so the training programme takes this level of fitness into account. He works eight hours a day, so training sessions have been designed to fit in after work. He could take part in one of these training sessions as part of his personal training, for example, he could take part in core stability training when he is with one of his clients, as well as plyometrics if that type of training is suitable for one of his clients.

Some key points are:

The FITT principles have been applied in designing this training programme:

- Frequency: training takes place five times a week in the first week and then goes up to six times a week in weeks 3 and 6.
- Intensity: one rep max increases for the weight lifted across the six-week training programme.
- Time: time for resistance-training sessions remains the same at 60 minutes, but time spent on plyometrics and core stability training over the course of the programme increases.
- Type: resistance exercises are used to increase strength, plyometrics to increase power and core stability to improve stability of the core.

Other principles of training also considered:

- Specificity: the training is specific to increase muscle strength and power.
- Overload: increase in % one rep max for weight lifted over the course of the six weeks.

- Progression: increase in % one rep max and time spent on plyometrics and core stability.
- Reversibility: sufficient time spent training each week to prevent reversibility from occurring.
- Rest and recovery: at least one rest day a week.
- Adaptation: will occur during the rest day. Upper and lower body are worked on alternate days to allow the muscles to fully recover before the next set of weight training.
- Variation: group exercise session has been included in week 1 with Pilates to support core stability training; in week 3, yoga has been added to add variation and to help with stress management. There is also the transition from fixed weights to free weights in week 3, which will require one spotter for weight training.
- Individual needs: the sessions take place in the gym and are specific to the clients' sporting needs.
- Periodisation: the training programme is a mesocycle to prepare the client for their sports competition. Each individual session is a microcycle, which will help to prepare Raj to be at peak performance on the date of the weightlifting competition.

Resources:

- free weights
- barbells
- dumb-bells
- person to act as a spotter for free-weight training
- fixed-resistance machines
- kettle bells – for core stability training
- access to Pilates and yoga classes
- medicine ball for core stability training.

Notes

Notes

Notes